Don't lose your mind

LOSE
YUR
WEIGHT

RUJUTA DIWEKAR

D0030106

EBURY
PRESS

EBURY PRESS

USA | Canada | UK | Ireland | Australia
New Zealand | India | South Africa | China

Ebury Press is part of the Penguin Random House group of companies
whose addresses can be found at global.penguinrandomhouse.com

Published by Penguin Books India Pvt. Ltd
7th Floor, Infinity Tower C, DLF Cyber City,
Gurgaon 122 002, Haryana, India

Penguin
Random House
India

First published by Random House India 2009

Copyright © Rujuta Diwekar 2009, 2015
Foreword © Kareena Kapoor 2009

All rights reserved

50 49 48 47 46 45 44

ISBN 9788184001051

Printed at Replika Press Pvt. Ltd, India

www.penguinbooksindia.com

This is for you, Bebo

Table of Contents

Preface

Dear readers,

Don't Lose Your Mind, Lose Your Weight, my first book, was published in 2009. It was written fast, over a few months, but the thinking behind it had taken many years of working as nutritionist and studying Ayurveda and yoga.

It's tough to revisit the past, especially when you are looking back at a pleasant memory or a discovery rather. For starters, I discovered that the call I received to write a book was not a hoax, it was real. But the most amazing and heart-warming discovery has been the generous love and the free marketing that the book has received from each one of you. Its success lies in the fact that it is your book, one that you have adopted, loved and promoted selflessly. A bestseller is made by readers and you have surely done a wonderful job at ensuring that this book sold year after year like, shall I say, hot jalebis on a Sunday morning.

Now to celebrate the completion of its sixth year in the bestseller charts, we have added a Q&A section that covers some of the most common myths and misunderstandings on food and weight loss still going around. I hope this will resolve any confusion you may have.

Lastly, the book couldn't have come this far without you and without the ever-enduring love and support of Kareena Kapoor. I remain hugely indebted to Bebo and to each one of you.

Happy reading—and happy eating.

Rujuta Diwekar
Mumbai, 2015

Foreword

For a long time, I used to think that diets were all about starving and punishing yourself. And I wasn't alone. A lot of people thought the same way.

Then I met Rujuta.

She totally changed my perception about diets and dieting. First, she told me it wasn't about starving but about eating well, eating right and eating regularly. I said, 'I'm a Kapoor, I love my parathas, paneer, cheese.' Rujuta replied, 'You can go right ahead and eat all of that and more.' I was like, cool, when can we start?

I started working with Rujuta around the time I started working on *Tashan*, and the results are there for all to see: my size zero became a subject of national interest. The media asked me if it was all diet, all exercise or both. My answer: it was seventy percent diet and thirty percent exercise (this through a combination of training and yoga).

Rujuta spent a lot of time understanding my work and my lifestyle, and gave me a diet totally customised to my needs. My diet on work days is different from my diet on shoot days, and even my shoot diets vary on days when I have a shoot or performance which requires dancing. Meals are planned according to level of activity.

When I am in Mumbai, breakfast is muesli and

milk, or a chilla or paratha (no chai or coffee)—when I was shooting in Ladakh, breakfast was fresh fruit and pudina chai without milk. In Ladakh, I also ate momos and thukpa (on the last day of the shoot I was even allowed a pizza!). I had appams and idlis in Kerala, and in Italy, it was risotto and pasta with gorgonzola (half portions though, not full).

I make sure I eat every two hours, and my meal or snack ranges from a sandwich to a glass of soy milk. For Rujuta focuses on nutrition and not just calories. Amazingly, she helps you keep the nutritional value of what you eat, as compared to how many calories you consume, high. And still enjoy what you're eating!

I have learnt what Rujuta means when she says, 'Be smart about food'. Now, thanks to her book, you can too. I'm certain you'll find it good enough to eat!

Kareena Kapoor
Mumbai, 2008

Introduction

I climbed the six kilometres of glacier from Gaumukh (at an elevation of 4000 metres) to Tapovan (4400 metres), with my heart beating in my ears with every step, expectations mounting. I'd heard so much about 'Simla baba', how he had been living in Tapovan for many years; the severe winters he had survived with snowfall more than six feet; how many penances he had done; and all starry eyed, I was hoping to learn something profound from him. On reaching Tapovan, I went to his hut immediately and asked him, 'Baba, aapko yahan kaun laya?'

'Jo tanne yahan laya, wohi manne yahan laya,' he replied, with a straight face. (He who brought you here, brought me here.) 'That's it?' I thought, disappointed.

It took me many more years and realisations to figure out that simplicity is profound.

Simplicity is profound

Don't lose your mind, by complicating something as simple as feeding yourself (although these words appear in smaller font on the cover, they are really the bigger message). Losing weight, as you will realise by the end of the book (I hope), is incidental. A by-product of following a common sense approach to eating—eating right.

But there is a thin line between simplicity and oversimplification. And just like you do with generalisations, you miss the point completely when you oversimplify. Eating a balanced diet will keep you healthy: a simple statement of fact. The less we eat, the thinner we become: an oversimplification. Other examples of oversimplification: blood group, GM (General Motors), cabbage soup and orange juice diets.

In a bizarre way, oversimplification seems to work best through mystification. Theoretically opposites, but apparently a potent combination. The best example of this combo: miracle foods. The weirder sounding, the better; Chia seeds, Acai berry, quinoa, etc, etc. We really want to believe that there is something miraculous in these 'exotic' foods, which will undo all wrong we have done to our bodies (oh we all know we have), but we have no idea how and we don't even want to know.

When I started as a nutritionist about ten years ago, I struggled to find my place in the fitness and wellness industry (hardly an industry, but nevertheless). For starters I had to deal with the stereotype of a healthy (as in plump and preferably double chinned, not fit and lean) sari and apron wearing dietician, while I was a young postgraduate in tights and jeans. My clients were aghast that I was promoting weight training, yoga and running as a means to keeping fit. 'Agar exercise karna hai, then why come to you?' asked a concerned, well-meaning client. Everybody wanted to know how much weight loss I could guarantee, or 'How much do you charge per kilo?' (I felt I was selling onions.) It was easier to fool people into believing that starvation was the way, somehow there was a ready clientele for anything like: no banana, no workout, no food only juice, etc. Where was the thrill in 'eating the right amount of food at the right time' as I prescribed? Yet as I struggled to find a foothold, I was sure that eventually people would realise (obviously with the help of some fitness professionals, more access to information and some hard hitting experiences) that losing fat and getting into shape has much more to it than how many grams or kilos you have dropped in a week or six months.

About this book

Through this book I share with you my take on dieting, and how dieting or diet is the most misunderstood term in English. **There is no such thing as going 'on' or 'off' your diet.** Eating correctly has to be a lifelong commitment, and the diet should be a reflection of this. This automatically rules out any extreme diet or crash diets which require you to go 'off' them. Diet, or what you eat, should be planned according to your activity, lifestyle, fitness levels, likes, dislikes, genetics, etc. It should be part of our daily life, just as brushing our teeth is. **For diets to work they have to be personalised.**

Oversimplification or generalisation has never worked. We are all genetically predisposed to carry fat in different parts of our body. So for fun, pick up the book which has the shape on its cover you identify with more, apple or pear (but do know that the basics of fat loss and healthy living remain the same, regardless of your shape, size, gender, age, nationality, etc).

My other belief (which you will find in this book) is that **all food is good**. All foods contain nutrients which have their own role to play in our body. We need all kinds of nutrients, like carbs, proteins, fats, vitamins and minerals, and depriving us of even one of them will create an imbalance in our system. Also, there is **no bravery attached to weight loss**. You can achieve it just by falling sick. What is most important is that you feel good about yourself, treat yourself well, **be committed to eating properly and exercising;** and weight loss, rather fat loss, will just happen. Punishing yourself by going on deprivation diets (liquid diets, low carb, high protein or any other fad diet) is never going to work. You will lose weight but at what cost? Not to mention that it will all come back, double of what you lost, in fact.

My book is about my philosophy of dieting which is a confluence of what I have learnt (and still am learning) in my studies of yoga and ayurveda, and during my Sports Science and Nutrition PG. Over the years I have come to understand that everything that we do or do not do is motivated by a strong desire to be happy. We want to lose weight because we think that it will make us happy. We want to, just have to, eat that pastry because it will make us happy. We don't want to eat karela sabzi because that will make us unhappy. The problem is that we are looking for happiness in the wrong place. Happiness is within us (clichéd but true) and when we get in touch with ourselves, our true being, we will discover happiness. Dieting or eating correctly, is a process, a learning tool, to go within. And when we see or experience that glimpse of reality within ourselves, it will (has to) reflect in our physical body.

Wikipedia on crash diets

A crash diet is a diet which is extreme in its nutritional deprivations, typically severely restricting calorie intake. It is meant to achieve rapid weight loss and may differ from outright starvation only slightly. They are not meant to last for long periods of time, at most a few weeks. Importantly, the term specifically implies a lack of concern for proper nutrition.

It is the last sentence above that is really scary. We just seem to lack that concern, that commitment to feed ourselves right. My clients often ask me what I feel about the so called expert dieticians, (or diet therapists, diet doctors, whatever), who are making people go on extreme diets in the name of 'guaranteed weight loss', spot reduction, improving metabolic rate and stuff like that? I think we are barking up the wrong tree here. It's a simple scenario of demand and supply. When people stop punishing themselves, fad diets will beat a quick retreat. That a lot of dieticians will find themselves out of a job is another issue altogether.

How to use this book

Using common sense when it comes to eating correctly is the central theme of the book. I have tried to put my view across in a way that all of us with or without a background in fitness and nutrition will understand. Throughout the book I have liberally used the experiences of my clients and the amazing stories they had to tell, as examples to illustrate my point better and to make it connect with you, my reader. I feel all of us will be able to relate at some level with these real life examples. Of course wherever required, I have used fictitious names.

At some places I draw parallels between food and subjects which may seem to be completely irrelevant or far removed from it such as politics or religion or our cars. But in my experience we seem to understand the politics of our country or the state of our car better than we do our body, hence the comparison. It is just my attempt to demystify diet and dieting.

Chapter 4, 'The four principles of eating right', is the cornerstone of my philosophy. It is the book in a nutshell.

Furthermore, for all the busy bees out there I have put a cheat sheet at the end of each chapter, summarising all the important points of the chapter. These are your takeaways.

I have used boxes all through the book for everything from exploding myths to relating interesting anecdotes, or to talk about anything supporting the text in the chapter. The box on crash diets is a case in point. I had the best time writing these boxes and hope you enjoy them as well, as you read and reread.

This book will urge you to think differently about your body, food, and the act of eating. At least that's what I want it to do. I sincerely hope it does. As for how much weight will you lose? Two things. First, know that every time you talk about weight loss, what you are actually trying to achieve is fat loss. Second, focus on the essentials: eating right and eating on time. Fat loss, remember, just happens. Once you follow the easy to understand and (surprisingly) easy to practice principles, you will notice that you feel different in as little as two weeks. You will get much more intuitive towards food, sleep better and feel much more energetic. In about three months you will see visible changes and drop a couple of sizes in clothes. You will also find that you naturally won't overeat, will understand how and when to eat that pastry, enjoy a sense of calm and peace and most importantly, stop worrying about how much you weigh.

Happy reading.

Rujuta Diwekar
Mumbai, 2008

1

What diet is not

My clients often ask me, 'You mean I can eat chutney with coconut, aloo paratha and puri bhaji? But where is the "diet" in this?' They sound almost disappointed. The word 'diet' has become synonymous with drastic weight loss, health loss, energy loss, metabolic rate loss and most importantly loss of sanity! **Diet has become a four letter word that it isn't.**

I strongly believe that your diet has to be a representation of what you will be eating your entire life. It has to remain true to your genes, your likes and dislikes, your work life, your level of activity, and only then does it have a good chance of working. Can you lead a life where you have papaya or dudhi juice all day long? If the answer is no, then don't go on that diet. **Diet is not starvation.**

A diet has to achieve much more than weight loss. Weight loss, or rather fat loss, is just one of the many wonderful side effects of changing your lifestyle. Dieting that has only weight loss as its primary goal is a failure even before you go on it. It's like some boot camp you go to, kill yourself at, and come back thinner. You are glad to be back home; and within four days of being back home you become healthy (read fat) again. The challenge is to keep up with the routine you kept at the boot camp but it is impossible given your working schedule, sleeping hours, responsibilities, practical issues. **Dieting is not about 'going on' a diet.**

Let's take a look at some of the popular diet fads and how they work against you.

Diet as punishment: the compensation diet

Real life example: 'Compensation diet! What's that?' I asked. 'What? [shocked, very shocked] You don't know?' I did the Indian way of nodding my head for, 'No, I don't.' Now I was at a south Mumbai gym where the owners where promoting me as a 'superb nutritionist from the suburbs'. And the lady who sat across from me was already feeling cheated because she had never thought that she would need to explain 'a compensation diet' to a dietician. Fortunately, she was a compassionate socialite. 'Rujuta, you should know your basics', she warned. 'Look, when you overeat and drink the night before, you visit a dietician the next morning and he or she can workout a compensation diet for you. Which means that the next day you eat very little or nothing and workout extra so that you can burn off everything you ate the previous night.'

'Or,' she went on, 'when you know that you have a big party tonight you just don't eat anything in the day. So you skip lunch but you can have low fat crackers, sukha bhel, tea and coffee, etc so that you can compensate for the night'.

Wow. 'I knew people did this,' I said, 'but I didn't know it was called the compensation diet'.

'You are a typical ghat [slang for Maharashtrian with limited or zero IQ but a big ego],' she joked.

Now it was my turn to speak. 'I call it crime and punishment. The crime: overeating. Punishment: deprivation of food. Our relationship with food shouldn't be about crime and punishment. We all overeat sometimes. So what? Fill it, shut it, forget it. Just get back to your normal workout and eating pattern from the next day. The body doesn't discriminate and store last night's calories in some special place so that next day when you kill yourself on the treadmill the body just exclusively burns that. And give yourself more space than this. It's ok to overeat once in a while, just don't carry the baggage forever. Get back to your diet plan from NOW.'

'Maybe you can say that because you can "afford" to eat,' said the socialite.

'So can you,' I assured her.

'I could die for a body like yours.'

'Great, but make sure you don't kill yourself by trying to compensate. Just get on with life. Just like if you sleep with somebody other than your partner you still get on with married life the next day, right?'

'You really are a ghat.'

Extreme diets just don't work: the detox diet

Most diets are impossible to keep at because they always advocate something extreme. Besides being

13

difficult to maintain, they're harmful for you physically and mentally. Let's talk about one of my all time favourites: the detox, weight loss and maintenance programme.

Oh! I love this one. 'Detox diet', the most fashionable term in dieting. So first you accept that everything you have fed your body is toxic, then you become a saint for a week and detox. And how? Using juices of course. And to punish yourself for being fat you use the yuckiest vegetables and make juices out of them: karela, dudhi, turiya, etc. You gulp them down with the bravery of a Kargil war soldier.

Real life example: Kareena once related a sad incident to me. A friend of hers was desperate to lose weight. She signed up for a programme with a very 'successful' dietician cum naturopath doctor who has the reputation of creating 'magic' in as little as 15 days. As Bebo and her friends sat at the dining table one day, the friend, who had already 'successfully' lost 7 kilos in 10 days, broke down. 'How,' she asked Bebo 'can you eat paneer?'

'I am losing because I am eating,' replied Bebo. But by that time her friend was sobbing uncontrollably. She had lost her weight but she had lost her energy and power of reasoning too. And why not? For the last week she had been on a diet of 4 glasses of dudhi juice and 3 oranges a day. What's worse, to deal with the headaches induced by starvation she had been advised to have 6 cups of tea or coffee. The girl's mother was obviously upset; her daughter

14

had blacked out twice in that week. But nothing could deter her from this detox diet. The next day the concerned mother called Bebo and asked her to give her daughter her diet secret.

This girl's diet of course would have to be planned differently from Bebo's, but one thing was for sure: she had to start eating.

Real life example: One of my clients (before she met me) visited a well known naturopath. The naturopath was popular because everything she recommended was from your kitchen. Of course there was no need to workout. (This is always sold as a special attraction. I think the whole plan is to keep clients dull and lazy.) The detox diet consisted of methi seeds and some kaju draksh soaked overnight and eaten first thing in the morning, followed by 2 figs, 2 walnuts, 2 pistas and an apple. Lunch was salad and a glass of buttermilk. Dinner was soup and a glass of milk with 4 different dried fruits. (2½ of each, soaked for 2 hrs and made into a paste. Mind you, not in the mixer but hand ground.)

'Wow!' I exclaimed. 'This sure is detox! So do you feel better or do you feel like the peel of a soaked almond?'

'Exactly,' exclaimed my client 'I feel like a peel— wasted and drained, for the last two days.' Now, dried fruits are great, but eating dried fruits almost exclusively is downright foolish.

So take my word for this: detox, like all other extreme diets, is a sham. At the end of these diets (they inevitably end) people's bodies and minds age and their metabolic rate is lower than ever before. So when they get back on the so-called 'maintenance diet' (usually similar to what they were eating before they went on the detox) all the fat starts creeping back, making their bodies look ugly (to them), and what it does to their confidence is indescribable. People who have put their bodies through this torture think of themselves as incapable of losing weight. Instead of understanding how much the diet has damaged their system from within they think they are not disciplined (because post crash diet the body goes in a tizzy, demanding calorie rich food), so they deserve to be fat!

Don't go for diet plans which deprive you of food or make you eat only one type of food. The point is to never regain the weight you have lost. For this to happen you have to understand how your body works and show the commitment to eat the right food at the right time. **This is going to be the major focus of this book.**

Everything 'herbal' is good—really?

Real life example: I met a woman recently, an investment banker, who took great pride in being in one of the top notch positions at one of India's leading banks. She had a supportive husband and 2 children, 3 years and 8 months old respectively. She had been forced to take a sabbatical after her mother-in-law had told her she could no longer look after her children while she 'made merry' at the bank. Though she doesn't hold anything against her mother-in-law, the banker decided she had to find some way to put her year-long break to good use. So she looked at her life and decided that the only area she was lacking in was a good body. She did what most sensible people in her position do: joined a gym and went on a diet, under the guidance of an 'expert' dietician. She lost all her weight, well most of it: 16 kilos in 6 months. Success story? Well, not quite. Her friends who met her after all this time looked at her and asked why she looked so dull. Her facial skin underwent a huge change, turned a few shades darker and pigmented in a few places, her nails chipped as she tried to open the zip of her Jimmy Choo, and her hair looked dry and coarse (in spite of a 2 week hair spa at one of the best salons in Bandra). She had also developed a little lump in her breast (thankfully non-malignant).

The banker had an analytical mind and was from one of the best business schools in India. But while she tried to understand why she needed to have various nutrient supplements in her diet and what their functions were, she never took the protein shakes and vitamins that her dietician recommended (because she thought the dietician was promoting gym business); however she happily took the herbal medicines because according to her, they are 'SAFE'.

Everything that is herbal is not necessarily safe. Nicotine and marijuana are herbal too. Regular users can vouch for their 'health benefits'!

While going on anything remotely herbal make sure that it matches your body constitution. Get the advise of a qualified ayurvedacharya or vaidya before popping pills or swallowing syrups. Ayurveda is a very complex science and it takes more than a lifetime to decipher it. A 3 month course in south India or Thailand doesn't make you a qualified practitioner, nor does saying vatta, kapha, pitta, or prana (ayurvedic terms) after every sentence, so stay away from the likes of these. (Finding a genuine ayurvedic doctor or vaidya in India is challenging enough; if you live abroad it is going to be next to impossible. I was once served puri, uncooked dal and a distorted version of khichdi as an ayurvedic meal by a high-end New York city yoga centre.)

What went wrong with my banker was that she worked out too much, ate too little and took herbal pills which altered her hormonal balance and thyroid levels. She asked questions about proteins, vitamins, minerals but never once doubted the authenticity of the herbal products.

Everything made in labs is not 'dangerous or artificial' and everything that's herbal is not 'safe'. In fact a lot of herbal products are made synthetically, in factories, or are cleaned, packaged or purified in factories, making them just as 'artificial'.

But it's not about natural or artificial, it's about knowing that the product you are using is safe for you. And you can know that only by going to the right professional and of course making sure that all your questions (however small or stupid) are answered in layman's language, with compassion and patience. Tip: carry a list of your questions and a pen or pencil with you. Tick off all questions as they get answered. Do not accept 'because I am telling you' as an explanation.

Exercise and dieting are mutually exclusive — no they aren't

Real life example: One day the receptionist at the gym where I used to consult came to me with an unusual request. A man had asked to see me, but he didn't want to go on a diet. He just wanted to talk! The receptionist wanted to check if I was ok with this. 'How does he look?' I asked. Was this just a ploy to line maaro me?

'No, no.' She assured me. 'His son is in the 8th standard and is working out in the gym too. He lost his wife recently and just wanted to discuss some health issues with you before committing to a diet.'

'Alright,' I told her. 'If you vouch for him I will see him but only for ten minutes.' (I had all the time in the world but was zealously learning to be a professional.)

'Hello madam,' the old man said. 'Thanks for seeing me. I just want you to look at me.' He then asked me what I thought his age was.

Now I was a smart girl and had learnt within months of setting up my consultancy NEVER to answer this question. 'Well I don't take guesses, why don't you tell me your age,' I said.

'I am 48.' Oops! He looked like he was 60. 'How much do I weigh?' Another question I had learnt not to answer.

'I weigh 68 kilos,' he told me. He looked 88 to 90 kilos to me. Then, he took out a *Bombay Times* paper cutting from his pocket. He pointed to a large advertisement for a chain of weight loss clinics which had a 'before' and 'after' picture of a man. 'Look, that's me.'

'Congratulations,' I managed. He looked like a super star in the pic as compared to what he looked like in reality. He was regarded as an inspiration to all the other clients at the centre, I was made aware, and the weight loss chain was flying him to Delhi to inaugurate their new franchise and hosting him at a five star hotel!

'That's great.' I said. But what did he want from me? 'I want you to come with me to the changing room and take a look at me.' What? This was the first time a client had asked to strip in front of me. (But it's not the only reason why this incident is memorable.) Having been in the fitness industry for over three years I was used to people describing their bodies, sex life, toilet rendezvous, etc in detail to me, but this was a first. I accompanied him to the men's locker room and he took his clothes off.

Flop! Out fell his stomach, towards his knees. 'This,' he held the jiggly wiggly mass in his hands. 'I want to get rid of this.' 'Alright, lets go out and talk,' I said. I managed to mask my emotions but I felt disgust and sympathy for him at the same time, and with alarming intensity. What had this man done and why?

'What have you been doing?' I asked. 'Well I weighed 116 kilos when I lost my wife a year ago. My son is in the 8th standard and it's very difficult for me to look after him alone. I am making very good money in my business and I want to remarry because my son needs a mother.'

'Really?' I said to myself. 'Well,' he said, 'nobody was going to marry a 116 kilos widower with a teenage son.' Friends and family asked him to lose weight. So he paid over a lakh at the weight loss centre and enrolled in a 6 month programme where all he had to do was lie down on a table for 20 to 30 minutes daily while painless electric currents worked on him, and go on a crash diet where he ate barely anything the whole day: channa, buttermilk and some dal. To speed up the process, he was asked to go on an hour long walk (no gym of course) every morning and evening, if he wanted faster 'results'. Then the centre suggested another programme: using firming gels for his belly. But after spending close to half a lakh for the gels and massage therapy, his stomach still sagged. So the centre suggested a tummy tuck, and asked him to increase the duration of his walks to 1½ hours, twice a day. 'I have started the walks but am not sure about the tuck. It will cost me a lot, and funnily I don't actually feel good being at 68 kilos. I always thought I would feel great even if I reached

80 kilos. I have never been so thin all my life, so why do you think I am not looking great after such successful weight loss?' (Incidentally, he had also lost most of his hair. For which the centre had an oil and massage programme of course, and a weaving programme too: he had signed up for the oil and massage programme already.)

I gave him a lecture on how he had lost all his lean body weight. 'Your bones must be hollow and your muscles have shrunk. You must start training with weights to rebuild lost muscle and bones. Of course you will need to go very slow. The diet plan that I put you on will be very different from what you have been following and will make you gain some weight. Are you ok with that?'

'Yes I am,' he pleaded, 'I just need to feel better.'

We ended the conversation with me warning him that he really shouldn't be walking so much—didn't he do any work in the day?

'I have good staff,' he said. 'But why do you want me to cut down on the walking?'

'Because,' I replied, 'your weight bearing joints are weak after the crash diet and not strong enough to bear the stresses that three hours of walking would place on them.' I asked if he really planned to go to the Delhi opening. 'This weight loss has done you no good.'

'I have good relationships with everybody at the centre and they have helped me achieve an impossible task [I was just beginning to understand what goes on inside the mind of a fat body] of losing weight so out of gratitude I will go.'

'But you will fool many others,' I argued.

'Yeah but...'

I left it at that.

A week later my receptionist told me that the man had called to cancel his appointment. 'Rujuta, that man won't come today. He went for a walk yesterday morning, tripped over a speed breaker, fell down, and suffered multiple fractures on his arm.'

'What?' So here was a man who had just lost a lot of lean weight: lack of exercise reduces neuromuscular control, while not eating in the morning and for long hours during the day reduces blood glucose levels. The combined effect of it all was that just tripping over a speed breaker, which at worst should have bruised his arm, left him with multiple fractures. The only good thing was that he didn't go for the Delhi opening!

Where is the bravery in losing weight? People with diarrhoea lose weight. So do people with jaundice, malaria, TB, not to mention cancer and AIDS. In fact the bigger the disease the faster the weight loss. Because we think that weight loss will make us happy, but we feel only frustrated and older (not wiser) at the end of yet another extreme diet, it comes with a heightened sense of victimisation and betrayal. The minute we are 'off' the diet all our weight is back. Please note that this time the weight gain is only in terms of fat weight. So our body composition is now worse than ever. We have lost our muscle and bone density, and our fat weight is higher than what it was when we went on the diet.

A lot of dieticians are popular because they guarantee weight loss without any exercise. So cool na? And some advertisements even top that. No diet, no exercise, no pills, only weight loss! If you are a regular on the Mumbai local (like me), you must have entertained yourself (with someone treading on your toes, an elbow in your breast and an umbrella poking in your back) by reading one of those ads: 'No boss, no timing, no paper work, no travel, no selling—earn up to Rs 100,000 per month.' What do you think of these ads? I think the same about no exercise, no diet, no pills, only weight loss ads.

Any programme which discourages you from exercising is worthless. Being on a diet might help you lose weight, but without exercise we lose our muscles and bone density. And loss of bone density and muscle is ageing. **The human body is designed for continuous activity.** The least we can do is give it 30 to 45 minutes of exercise for 3 days a week to keep it in good shape and condition. The body works on one basic principle: use it or lose it. Humans were born with a tail remember? We lost our tail because we never used it. We might soon lose out on our muscles and bone density, as we just don't seem to use either of these live tissues.

I hated maths in school. But loved one word: corollary. It's used in algebra all the time. Ok, so here is the corollary to the above myth: as long as you exercise it's ok to eat whatever you want. Really think so? Do you think as long as you drive your car it doesn't matter what you put into it; kerosene, petrol, diesel? (People are always so much smarter about their cars than their bodies.) Nope. Wrong! Now just because I use my body regularly doesn't mean I should abuse it. So, exercise is a part of adopting a better lifestyle but it is NOT an alternative to eating right. In fact the more people get committed to working out, the more they usually care about how to get the right nutrients to their body.

When you start eating healthy and exercising regularly, you will initially see a drop in your body fat but not as much in your weight. However, when you crash diet, you lose a lot of weight because your lean body weight comes down while your fat body weight remains the same, and sometimes actually increases. Fat occupies a lot of volume on the body and weighs very little. Muscle, is denser, so it occupies much less space but will weigh a lot. (Compare fat to 1 kilo cotton and muscle to 1 kilo iron. Can you see what I am saying? Same weight but big difference in their volume or the space they occupy.) This is why people often look flabby after their 'diets'. So stop holding your body for ransom on the weighing scale. Why do you need to know how much you weigh? It is no indicator of health or fitness levels. Know that the higher the amount of lean body weight you carry, the greater your fat burning capacity. Do you really want to go for 'guaranteed' weight loss (invariably attacking the LBW) and lose your fat burning abilities?

Why your scales lie

Your body weight is made up of 2 parts: the fat weight and the lean body weight. The lean body weight is the weight of your bones and muscles. The fat weight is exactly what it says it is. Never look at the weighing scales and judge your health. The thing to look at is the fat weight (and how much fat there is in your body, ie the fat percentage) rather than your total body weight. Serena Williams, for example, might have a high body weight (because of her high lean body weight) but has a very low fat percentage. The *FTV* models might weigh less on the scale and appear skinny but some of them have fat percentages as high as 30%. The ideal fat percentage should be under 20% for men and under 25% for woman. This is also why you should **never judge your health by BMI** (body mass index = weight (kg)/height $(m)^2$) because BMI is just about total body weight. BMI doesn't take into account the contribution of fat weight towards your total weight. (2 people with the same BMI can look drastically different because of the difference in their fat percentages. The person with high fat percentage will look flabby and weak while the one with low fat percentage will look lean and toned.)

Measuring body composition

Dual energy X-ray absorptiometry, DXA (previously known as DEXA), is a great way to measure body composition (though this was never its original purpose). It will not just tell you how much body fat you carry, but also the density of your bones (very important to know the conditions of your bones if you want to lead a pain free life and wish to look toned and age gracefully).

The most accurate fat measurement is under water weighing, but that's complicated and DXA is relatively inexpensive, accessible and quick.

DXA scans are available at most multi specialty hospitals or investigation clinics. All machines have an inherent error and need to be calibrated regularly. So, make sure you measure yourself on the same machine every time (or at least one made by the same manufacturer) to account for mechanical errors, if any.

Body fat table		
Description	Women	Men
Essential fat	12 - 15%	2 - 5%
Athletes	16 - 20%	6 - 13%
Fitness	21 - 24%	14 - 17%
Acceptable	25 - 31%	18 - 25%
Obese	32% +	25% +

Note: this doesn't state your body weight. If less than 25% of your weight is coming from metabolically inactive fat tissue, then whatever your total body weight may be {metabolically active tissues: bone, muscle, organ, water, etc, (ie everything other than fat) + metabolically inactive tissue, (ie fat)}, that is fine.

One size doesn't fit all

Real life example: I met an art promoter at a Sunday brunch. Smart, articulate, sensitive, nose pierced, long bandhani skirt with a noodle strap top, flabby arms hidden under a stole (a walking Fab India advertisement) and thick kohl around her sparkling eyes to take attention away from the chubby cheeks.

'Listen, tell me what to do? Everybody is talking about you these days,' she said to me, pointing towards the stretch marks which started from her chest and went all the way down her arms, and which she was trying so hard to hide with her stole. 'I always wanted a body like yours.'

'Thanks,' I said. (I always thank.)

'I do yoga regularly,' she told me.

'Superb,' I remarked.

'What's the use?' she asked, frustrated by my remark. 'Look at my arms, I would love to wear this without the stole but you know I can't. I just can't.'

Once again, I inadvertently found myself slipping into the counsellor's role. 'You have got to watch your diet, exercise alone means nothing.' Ha, now I had gone where I shouldn't have.

'Hey, I have tried everything. For the last three months all that I have been eating is papaya in the morning, salad and egg white for lunch, chicken breast and soup for dinner.' She was turning papaya pink now. 'I am constipated, frustrated, hungry all the time and I am organising an exhibition next Sunday. So I am neck deep in shit. This is my big daddy of all exhibitions and look at me. I am looking like... like... ' she searched for words.

'Stale pizza with all the toppings,' I said, completing her sentence. (Thankfully not loudly.) Then, she took her glass of wine and hid it behind her back, and continued, 'Ok with the exception of this glass of wine I have been very clean. But my weight has not moved, not even by 200 grams.' (How and why people track weight by grams will remain a mystery to my mind). Ok now I was in a spot, I had to talk, give my 'expert opinion', and everybody at the brunch wanted to listen to it. What do you say to somebody who is so angry and frustrated with her diet and herself? Anything that you can say is wrong and hopelessly inappropriate.

I put my hands on her shoulders. 'Relax,' I gestured.

'What have I done to myself? Some of my buyers and friends recommended high protein so I went on it ya,' she said controlling the tears now and doing a damn good job of it.

'It's your body, it deserves much more respect than this,' I said. 'And I think you are a great looker, you just need to put some zing back into your food and life. I don't even think that you are fat.'

'It's just some 4 to 5 kilos and I want to lose that.'

'They are always the hardest to lose,' said one of the onlookers, witnessing this whole drama. (The brunch was successful, everybody had a story to go back with now.)

'Hey, I need to get water proof kohl,' said the art promoter, quickly gathering herself. Everybody laughed. Tension eased. Thank God.

My heart goes out to all those who try out everything that appears on the net, glossies and the grapevine. Dieting is not rocket science but it's a science in itself. Doing random things with food and dieting will always backfire. I really think that we treat our cars with much more respect than we treat ourselves.

This is a very important piece of advice for all my readers: never, ever 'just try' diets that your over-enthu friends, clients, etc swear by. It may have worked for them (I doubt it though), but it's not necessary that it will work for you. People who really care about the diet they are on will always ask you to consult their nutritionist or dietician. When it comes to diets, it's not one size fits all. Diets needs to be personalised and customised to your needs, fitness levels, exercise frequency, profession, climate, and your tastes in food. What this book aims for is to try and take your present day eating habits and improve them: you are going to have to create your own diet plan. All I'll do is give you the few ground rules to help you through it.

The truth about low fat and sugar free alternatives

Real life example: 'Arre kya kar rahe ho? Accha idhar rakh do,' said Karisma, as she hid a plastic bag behind the sofa she was sitting on.

'What are you hiding?' I asked.

'Nothing ya. Shit, I was sure you would ask.'

'Show me,' I gestured.

Sheepishly, she pulled the bag out from behind the sofa. It was overflowing with all the fat free, low fat, sugar free things in the world. Low fat chips of all varieties; soy, nachni, methi, you name it. Baked chaklis, sugar free drinks aerated and non aerated.

'Who are you trying to fool?' I demanded.

'Nobody, ya. Why these are good of course. All my friends are having it.' Now in the make up mode, Lolo opened a packet of her baked chaklis and offered them to me. 'Try Rujuta, you will love them.'

'Oh come on, you obviously know you are doing something you shouldn't be, that's why you were hiding it from me.'

'Come ya, they are baked.'

So? I took a chakli and handed it to Karisma. 'Ok, break it. Now, keep the pieces down and look at your finger. What do you see?'

As the sun set on the Arabian Sea it reflected on Lolo's finger, and something shone on the tips of her fingers. 'No!! Shit ya!!'

'Come on, what do you see?'

'Oil. Yup, fat droplets.' That, sadly was an

abrupt end to her romance with low fat, low sugar, baked products.

Low fat snacks like baked chaklis, fat free ice creams, fibre loaded biscuits, etc are nothing but junk food coated with misinformation and some sharp marketing brain trying to sell them to a gullible audience which will bite onto anything that's fat free.

Now try a fun experiment. Just look at who is eating the low fat or sugar free variety. You will find that people who are already fat are eating this junk. They would actually be better off eating full fat ice cream, fried chaklis and cream biscuits. Because at least then you are aware that what you are eating is junk, so you limit the quantity that you consume. And seriously if you have just 1 or 2 chaklis or 1 or 2 cream biscuits once or twice a week, this won't get in the way of your losing weight. But eating this fat free or sugar free junk daily surely hampers your process of weight loss. No wonder then that all people buying fat free or sugar free junk are struggling to lose weight.

So should you not eat them at all? Of course you can eat them, but eat them knowing that they are just as harmful as the full fat, full sugar, fried items. Sometimes even more. Karisma confessed that she was dabaoing the chips and chaklis thinking they were healthy and could never make her fat. Similarly, when we eat these products, we invariably don't exercise caution because they are low fat. But low fat doesn't mean it won't convert to body fat. Also, most low fat foods are barely 1 or 2 grams lower in fat than full fat versions.

The worst thing is that most of these products use trans fat, which provides the right texture to food, makes it last longer and at the same time make you fatter and clog your arteries; also making you prone to heart diseases.

If you must eat chakli or chips make them at home and fry them. You will use good oil and eat your goodies hot, so they will taste better and also be nutritious. Since this is a long process you will land up doing this may be once a fortnight or once a month. Baked products, on the other hand, can be easily bought and stored so you have access to them almost daily. The choice is yours: get rid of repackaged junk food from your house.

The bitter truth about sweeteners

Should you be replacing sugar with a sweetener? Especially if you are diabetic or trying to lose weight? The answer clearly is NO. Why? Isn't it calorie free, a blessing for diabetics, and a great way to maintain a good figure? Yes, if you believe the marketing and advertising surrounding these sweeteners. No, if you are asking me to be straight up.

Sugar free chocolates, sugar free mithais, sugar free drinks, and almost every product that has the suffix diet attached to it has these sweeteners; as in most 'diet' drinks, 'diet' ice cream, diet yogurt, the list is endless.

While I was writing this book at Costa, I discovered yet again how most fat people asked for 'sweetener' over sugar and then had the sugar loaded biscotti which came free with the coffee, sometimes even asking for another helping. This is exactly what sweeteners do; they make your drink, yogurt, tea or coffee, etc zero on calories. This confuses the body, which demands calorie dense food almost immediately. Do you see the connection: diet drinks (free refills, sometimes) with calorie dense pizza and burger; biscuit with tea or coffee? Are you trying to avoid calories or fast carbs here? Clearly you are not succeeding, because you land up eating not just high glycemic index carbs, but also trans fats, and that's a lethal combination.

In all fairness, one time use of a sweetener will not harm you, but regular use is like a slow mo (sadistic) way of harming your body. (Another way of punishing ourselves for being fat?) Regular use of all sweeteners is associated with certain type of cancers, thyroid malfunction, memory loss, acidity, obesity, etc. And really, 1 to 2 teaspoons of sugar (even regular use) is not going to harm you as much as the sweetener.

Is it really so difficult to understand (and accept) that the only way to lose body fat is to eat right and at the right time, and to exercise regularly? No pill or powder, much less sweetener, can burn body fat or miraculously melt your fat away. Use your brains, stop living in the bubble.

So aspartame or no aspartame, get that sweetener out of your tea. All sweeteners will help you in only one way: in gaining weight.

All food is good

Glorifying or demonising any food item might be glamorous (and bread and butter) to many, but it's just not correct to do so.

A lot of 'experts' think fruits are great and will recommend that you have loads daily. Many of you must have been advised that instead of a dessert post dinner you are better off eating fruits. I know families who routinely cut apples post dinner and eat them thinking that it's the best thing they can do. Among fruits too, some are deemed evil and some angels. Almost all dieticians in India tell you that bananas, custard apples, chickoos and grapes are fattening, and orange, papaya, watermelon are low fat. Sometimes, when a myth has been around long enough it becomes the truth. Like the jhoppad pattis in Mumbai. Illegal—yes. Land grabbing—of course. But if they are around long enough, the slum dwellers own the land and politicians fight to get them legal status, water, electricity, ration card, etc.

Cut to fruits. Updating ourselves with the latest developments in nutrition science is something all of us nutritionists owe to ourselves and our clients. A few years ago, it was discovered that fructose (the sugar we get from fruits) gets converted to triglycerides (especially when eaten on a full stomach), a type of fat which circulates in our blood stream. High levels of triglycerides are responsible for heart disease, insulin insensitivity and of course lead to bigger fat cells. And our body is truly secular:

it treats all fructose equally. It doesn't matter which fruit you eat, it will surely give you fructose. So eat your fruit, but don't think that it's safer than eating a dessert. Its nutrients only work for us if we eat it at as a meal by itself: as a morning meal or after exercise, and not as a dessert after dinner.

Juices

We have teeth and gums which are meant for chewing food. Making a juice out of vegetables and fruits (no matter how fresh the fruit, or how expensive your juicer) robs you of all their vitamins and minerals. And even if you retain the fibre or add the fibre back to your juice, you have destroyed its structure. You are now drinking coloured water which has lost its nutrients; because the surface area of the fruit has increased, and exposure to the air and surroundings has already oxidised its nutrients. Fruits contain antioxidants. Ideally, they should get oxidised in your body and not outside it.

Eating a fruit is a better bet any day. It retains all the vitamins and minerals, chewing it provides a nice massage to your gums, and the fibre works at cleaning out your cavities. When it comes to fruit—eat, don't drink.

The other example is soy. There was a time when soy was the 'it' food, the miracle cure for everything from mood swings, weight gain and heart disease. There was such a soy craze that one doctor slash dietician made a killing selling everything from soy chakli to soy atta, soy cake, soy biscuits, soy milk, soy curd, soy water, etc. Did people lose weight? Of course they did, drastic amounts. But then some of the people who had been on this plan for a long time started developing medical conditions. They suffered from stretch marks, high triglyceride levels, depression, even cancer. Then everybody was quick to blame soy. This was about the same time there were reports linking soy to breast cancer. The problem here is that we have lost our ability to see things in totality. The clients suffered from this condition not because of soy but because they cut all other nutrients from their diet. They received no nutrition from any other food groups because they were overdoing the very healthy soy.

There is still no concrete evidence linking soy to breast cancer, but what is beyond doubt is that cancer is more likely in people with stress, little or no exercise, and whose diets are poor in nutrients but rich in calories.

Have you ever bought a car or bike? Or you must have at least seen ads which claim a mileage of 14 kilometres per litre for a new car. But when you buy the car and start driving, it gives you 10 kilometres per litre. You are still happy right? Because we use a lot of common sense with our car. If the ad says 14, then we know 10 is good. We all understand what the * which says 'under lab conditions', means. Under lab conditions you can prove almost anything you fancy. But what happens to your research in real life is a different story altogether.

So, use your common sense before you start replacing all your regular meals with just soy or papaya, or whatever the in thing is.

Whether we are talking about fruits or soy or

some other miracle food, one thing is for sure: if there are reports glorifying it today, in a couple of years there will be reports of it harming you. What is your option? Eat according to the latest flavour of the season? Nope, the only logical solution is to use the magical word: MODERATION. And, of course, common sense. If soy is great, use it but be careful not to replace everything with soy. Have it judiciously, maybe one serving a day, and talk to your body and stomach. If your body is taking to it nicely, stay with it. If not, forget it.

To summarise: there is really nothing like 'safe food' or 'fattening food'. Everything that you eat judiciously, at the right time and in the right quantity, is good for you. All foods provide us with specific nutrients which play a unique role in our body or metabolism. When we demonise one food type or glorify another, we completely miss the point. I'll talk about this much more deeply in 'What to eat', where I dissect all the 5 major nutrients for you. Hopefully by the end of this book you'll understand that all foods help us burn fat—even fat.

What's the solution?

So the best solution is to never go on a diet. Seriously. If I am saying this as a dietician, I either have gone bonkers or I am talking about some groundbreaking gene therapy. But it's none of the above. The reality is that for permanent changes in your body and to stay lean all your life (or even bikini-ready), you have to make sure that you never 'go' on a diet. Get the diet to grow on you instead. In other words, modify your lifestyle, ie eat right, exercise and think right about yourself. Crash dieting is like a fling with a bad boy (even when you are in it, you know it's not going to work long term); and modifying your lifestyle is like being in a loving and committed relationship (it might get boring sometimes, but it's the key to your mental and physical wellbeing). Trust me, adopting a healthy lifestyle is not as difficult as staying loyal in a marriage or loving your partner for a lifetime. It's much *more* difficult because it means unconditional love and acceptance of your own self and of your body.

I believe that people gain weight and then punish themselves with extreme diets because of an unhealthy attitude towards their bodies and towards food. In fact I interview any new client for 2 to 2½ hours before I plan their diets with them, because I believe that before they can change their eating habits they need to change their thinking—and for that I need to know how their minds work.

In *Don't lose your mind, lose your weight*, I will look at the way we all fall into the wrong eating patterns and false conceptions of what food is good and bad for us. In fact, I hope that when you get to the end of this book you'll realise that there is no such thing as right or wrong food. It all depends on how and when we eat it. You can actually eat your aloo parathas and not worry about the weight gain. All you really need to do is relearn how to eat, know how your body works and follow the four easy principles that I think are the cornerstone of correct eating.

Through the next few chapters my endeavour is to educate you about the different kind of nutrients and their functions in our body, how to manipulate their quantity to adjust to your lifestyle, and how to get a lean and toned body.

Cheat sheet

- Don't ever go on extreme diets—they're not sustainable and just don't work.
- Dieting should not involve starving yourself: you must eat to lose weight.
- Don't make angels and demons out of different foods: they're all just as good or bad for you.
- Just as everyone is different, everyone's diets have to be different too. Don't try someone else's regime.
- Make sure you know what's in low fat or sugar free foods; they aren't all that healthy, and shouldn't be consumed in excess.
- Exercise is non-negotiable. Unless you exercise, you'll never see enough of a result, despite all your good eating habits.
- Never go on a diet: modify your lifestyle.

2

How to eat: relearn

Know thy stomach

Ok, what do we know about our heart? We know that it's the size of our fist, and it's located inside our chest, slightly to the left side. It provides blood to the entire body. Also when we don't exercise or gain weight, our heart experiences stress. Fine, good enough. Now what do we know about our lungs? That they are inside our ribs and smoking can harm them. And regular exercise can improve their health. They provide O_2 to the body and throw out CO_2. Great.

Now, what do we know about our stomach? Do we know the size of our stomach? Its location? What it does for us? What can harm it? Surprisingly, though our stomach is an involuntary organ just like our heart and lungs, not too many of us seem to know much about our stomachs. We can guess that it is somewhere roughly between our chest and hips, that it is separate from the intestine (made up of the large and small intestine: the large is actually small and the small is large, almost 4000 square metres in area).

Why do we pay so little attention to our stomach? Is it because it never attacks us? We have all heard of heart attacks but stomach attacks? No. Our stomach never seems to attack us. (The word heart attack also is a misnomer. The heart is working for us from the time we are in our mother's womb. It is in fact one of the first organs that is developed, somewhere around the 6th week of pregnancy. The heart that we owe our life to cannot possibly attack us. But we definitely attack it with our habits, eating, lack of activity and exercise, etc. And then like the case of ulta chor kotwal ko daante, we call it heart attack.)

I think we care so little about our stomachs and digestive system because any amount of abuse to it doesn't lead to our death. At the most it's a week off from work. I know people whose stomachs are always crying out loud for attention with acidity, bloating, constipation, burps, farts, nausea, etc. But they are just not bothered to listen to its signals. Antacids, salts and laxatives have become a way of life for these people, almost a daily ritual.

Heard the term, 'stomach an insult'? We actually share a very abusive relationship with our stomachs. We eat all the junk in the world and then go on a 'detox' holiday. We come back from the detox holiday and get back to junk eating with a vengeance. Worse still, we go on crash diets consisting only of juices with guaranteed weight loss and then gain all the weight (sorry, double) back in 2 weeks flat. Some others let their body weight yo-yo as a way of life. Wedding? Party? Get thin. Over—get fat again.

Why do we do this to ourselves? Do we really hate ourselves so much? On the surface we do seem to care for ourselves. We wear good clothes, go for that manicure, get ourselves the best car and house that our money can buy, expect love and respect from our partners, etc. But if we love ourselves so much, why do we abuse that integral part of our system which provides us with love and nourishment; our digestive system?

If we want to get toned, muscular and popular, fit into that little black dress, have no stretch marks or be bikini ready 24/7, then we need to establish a good relationship with our stomach. One of mutual love and respect.

Loading the stomach when it has no capacity to digest is criminal. It's a human rights violation. Our lifestyles, where we eat nothing until evening and then start loading our stomachs for dinner, are just wrong. Its like hiring people for a 9 am to 5 pm job and giving them little or no work till 5pm—and then, just as they are about to leave from work, loading them with all the files and work in the world. You don't need me to tell you that these kinds of bosses receive no love or respect from the staff. Not that such a boss loves or respects the staff either. Such behaviour just leads to loss of productivity, time, creativity and basically loss of health of the organisation.

Extrapolate this to our eating habits. As the sun goes down, so does our digestion and assimilation ability. And we give our stomach no work and therefore no nourishment during the day. Its ability to digest food is highest between 7 am to 10 am, and many of us give it chai, coffee, cigarettes instead. Thus we actually work at making our stomachs dull and our digestive enzymes weak. We barely grab our lunch, and generally eat light till 5 pm. After that, as the stomach starts winding down and wants to rest, we load it with bhel puri, sev puri, grilled sandwiches, some more tea, coffee and cigarettes. Later between

9.30 and 11.30 pm, when the stomach is already tired and sick after the evening's snack attack, we give it a heavy dinner of pasta or rice with sabzi and chapati, and of course our favourite dessert. (Because dessert tastes best with dinner and we eat a lot for dinner because that's the only time the entire family eats together. That the centre of attraction during dinner is our darling TV is another story.) And so our stomach takes this abuse and ill treatment day in and day out, for years together. Then if it calls out to us for help by bloating, farting or burping, we think it is weak and not behaving well! And to suppress its cries of help we use antacids and laxatives.

Some go one step further and eat antacids and salts with their meals thinking they are nipping the revolt at the bud. Smart advertising professionals have made some interesting ads encouraging this behaviour. Remember the one where the son-in-law cannot eat beyond 4 or 5 laddoos, which are thrust upon him? Out comes the magic effervescent salt. Like a true hero he gulps them down and readies his stomach for more onslaughts. 'Ab sasural jaane ka koi tension nahi.' Wow, this son-in-law is every mom-in-law's dream come true because he dabaos everything that she cooks for him.

There have been times when during my meetings, my clients burp and I can write the entire diet recall down myself. The burp smells of samosa, kadhi, bhaji, everything. It's all just sitting there undigested for the world to smell. Some wise person rightly said, why fart and waste, when you can burp and taste? If you eat at a time when there are hardly any digestive juices being secreted, when the stomach has lost its power of digestion, when there is no prana (life force) in the stomach and when the mind is distracted, how can you expect food to get digested properly? And instead of the constant onslaught of antacids and laxatives, shouldn't you just learn to eat right and at the right time?

US bombed Afghanistan and Iraq, which created much more damage than any good. After that it wants to send aid to both these countries. No wonder the Afghanis, Iraqis and the Muslim world at large hates America. Make up your mind, America. Either stop bombing them or stop the aid. And chances are that once the bombing stops, they won't need the aid either. In the same way, if your overeating stops you won't need any digestion aid.

Fasting: yoga's take

Fasting is a powerful tool as a spiritual practice, but nowadays is used mainly as a weight loss tool by 'experts'. It is recommended by 'health experts' as a form of rest for the digestive system. Have you ever thought of giving your heart a rest? No? Then why think of the digestive system as something that needs rest? The digestive system, like the heart, is an involuntary system (designed for continuous activity), and to keep it in a relaxed state what we need to do is eat a little at a time. Yoga is, in fact, counter to some people's beliefs, against any extremes; including fasts. And of what use is a fast when all you think about is food? According to yoga the mind and body are interlinked. So even if you think about food and eating, you will see immediate effects in the physical body. This means that even thinking of chocolate pastry can lead to weight gain!

Overeating and overeating threshold

According to ayurveda, overeating is the cause of all diseases. **Overeating can be defined as eating more than the body's ability to digest at that point of time.** It doesn't simply mean eating the wrong foods, or eating too much. If the stomach lacks the fire or the power to digest at a particular time, then even a slice of an apple will amount to overeating. So overeating doesn't just mean eating a large quantity of food, it means eating that food at the wrong time.

Agastya Muni, one of the highly revered seers of India, once drank the entire ocean! You can actually eat all you want but you need to have the power to digest it. This means that your digestive fire should be active and efficient. You can keep the fire active through a disciplined lifestyle, regular exercise and optimistic attitude. Our basic problem today is that our digestive capacity (or fire) is diminishing and our consumption is increasing.

The overeating threshold is a very very thin line. That gap between eating the right amount and overeating is crossed by just one mouthful, bite or spoonful. It's crucial to be very aware of this threshold because once you cross this laxman rekha, then you can go on and on and on. Your senses go numb and you can eat up to 5 to 6 times your stomach's capacity. Obviously you know the inevitable consequence of this: you wake up dull, tired, bloated, and irritable the next morning. Sorry, forgot to mention this, but it's also a foolproof way of gaining body fat.

Let me give you two examples of how we often cross the overeating threshold without realising.

Example 1. Last night I had a friend over for dinner and we had a simple, wholesome meal of dal, paneer sabzi and roti. My friend had finished her meal, but I wanted another half piece of roti. My maid served the remaining half to my friend so as not to waste it. Priya didn't want to eat anymore but she ate that extra half without thinking and just like that, she crossed her overeating threshold. Often, we ask for that extra helping of our favourite dal or chicken curry although we know internally that we've finished our meal. And every time we do this, we've crossed our laxman rekha. Women often gain weight when they get married. It's because eating with someone else leads us to exceed our usual capacity, although most brides are quite unaware of this change because they're still eating less than their husbands.

Example 2. You are at the Marriot or Grand Hyatt or at some wedding and a huge buffet is laid out in front of you. When you look at the delicious food all around you, you can't help wondering how anybody could ever do justice to this fabulous spread. But you start off by being good, picking up only the salads, sabzis, and a few grilled or tandoor items, at the most half a roti or some pasta. As you get done with your food, one of your friends comes by with some yummy looking dessert on his plate. You are absolutely full and not feeling like it, but the dessert looks too yummy and the expression on your friend's face proves it. So you decide to have just a teeny weenie bite from your friend's plate. Ummm… it's delicious. You are experiencing a sensory overload and now you have crossed the laxman rekha. You find yourself marching towards the dessert counter. You help yourself to 3 or 4 desserts and of course a whole piece of that yummy looking pastry. Back at your table, you gobble down all of the desserts on your plate.

The sensory overload and deep sense of pleasure in the example lasts only for a while. What remains is the deep sense of guilt and shame at not stopping at that half piece of kaju katri or pastry. But when you ate that half piece, you had already crossed the overeating threshold. Everything after that happens so fast that you don't get the chance to stop or to apply your analytical mind and reasoning. It's like an accident. You can see the damage but you don't know what exactly happened.

The only way to avoid these diet accidents is by learning to observe our feelings and accepting them. So in situations like this, accept that you get tempted by pastries or kaju katri but refrain from actually eating them. No half piece or small bite, because after that it's just a downward spiral. Sadly, in spite of repeated experiences we simply refuse to learn from our past.

Tip: don't store sweets or fried foods at home. You might be gifted mithai and the like at festival time. After completely enjoying 1 or 2 pieces, give these away to friends, family, share it at office, give it to your watchman, bai, etc.

Post tip: don't always dump your excesses on one person. Choose different people for charity. But get those things out of your sight and reach.

Eating as a way to overcome boredom or entertainment

Watching a movie? Eat popcorn. Stuck in a party with nobody interesting? Nibble on the deep-fried starters. Bored of eating the same old dal, sabzi, roti? Call for a pizza. Not happy with your sex life? Eat a pastry. Too often we use food as a crutch to overcome boredom or as a distraction from our deep rooted fears or feelings. This is also what girly magazines call 'comfort food'. Food, or the act of eating, is the most primitive form of comfort, but we need to understand that food is about providing nourishment to the body and not about overcoming boredom or stale relationships. And have you noticed that when you eat food as entertainment or as a distraction from some niggling thought, it's always something that is calorie dense, extremely sweet or extremely salty?

And no, your boredom or thoughts don't go away after eating that pastry or chips, in fact they are still very much there. So what are you going to do? Reach for another one?

Real life example: Siddharth, my cousin, had gained notoriety amongst family and friends for eating till he almost choked. And he would eat everything from paneer tikkas, Schezwan rice, puri bhaji, dal, rice, noodles, you name it. He would stuff himself till he was full, his body chock-a-block from mouth to anus. After eating he would feel dull, slothful, tired, sleepy. He suffered from regular migraine attacks, and had observed that if he went hungry migraine would set in. So he took to stuffing himself to prevent migraine and this only made it worse (of course). He wouldn't be able to focus on work and would lose out on the entire day. Siddharth is a workaholic by the way, so anything other than losing a day's work would have been acceptable. He had joined his father's business and had taken it to another level altogether. But along with that he took his waist, body weight and cholesterol levels sky high too.

Last year, the news that he was about to have his second child, spurred him to seriously do something about his weight. And because I was now his favourite star's (KK's) dietician, he took me seriously as well. He choked with emotion when I told him he could continue having his rotis with ghee, cheese, paneer, paratha, koki and sindhi kadhi (married to a Sindhi, he loves the stuff).

I got Siddharth to start eating more slowly, and to serve himself smaller portions, the rule being that he served himself half of what he would normally eat. Then I got him to follow my 4 principles, and eat small meals every 2 hours. So Siddharth went from overeating to eating just right. (Men are blessed. They have loving wives who go all the way to support them in their diet and workout routines. Shalu, Siddharth's wife, packed 6 dabbas a day and instructed the driver, bai and office boy to remind sahib, every 2 hours, to eat. And she did all this through her pregnancy, that too with a two year old son to take care of).

And what a journey that was. From no workout at all to working out three times a week, 2 mammoth meals a day to 7 light meals a day, 98 kilos to 82 kilos, 38 inches to a 30 inch waist, Siddharth has come a long way and so have his eating habits. Today he is the most energetic dad for his lovely boys, much more successful in his business, and most importantly has lost all interest in overeating. Friends and family can't believe what they are seeing when they see him stopping at 2 chapatis. 'I just can't eat more than this,' he confesses, 'my stomach's shrunk!'

Learning to train your stomach

Is it possible to shrink your stomach? Yes, it is. But for that, just like Siddharth, you have to relearn your eating habits.

What's the biggest thing that we have to learn? The biggest lesson that we have to learn is to stop eating before reaching the overeating threshold. Now the question is, how do we stop before we reach the overeating threshold? And how do we recognise it?

The overeating threshold is different for different people. And even in the same person it changes with age, stress, exercise, time of the day, season, etc. But no, it's not complicated to find your own threshold. You won't need a blood, urine or stool test.

The secret to staying within the threshold is to have more small and frequent meals (more on that in Chapter 4, 'The 4 principles of eating correct') like Siddharth. But what do we mean by small? The stomach is actually the size of 2 palms. The food it can take at a time is the amount that fits in your 2 palms. Have you seen pictures of Buddhist and Jain monks, cupping their hands together for alms and food? Well, in an ideal world, that's the amount of food our stomach should take in at a time. By constantly eating beyond our capacity, however, we stretch the stomach and take in more food than it can digest. This is why I advocate small, frequent meals. Give the stomach a dose of what it needs. When it's finished digesting, give it some more. You're still giving your stomach plenty of food; you're simply lengthening the process of feeding yourself. Siddharth was still eating a lot and not giving up any of his favourite foods, but by cutting the quantities down and eating through the day, he had cut down on the overeating.

However, most of us may not be able to stick to the ideal measure of food, at least not initially. Also, often we are at restaurants and parties and can't always control the amount we get on our plates. And as I've said, your threshold will vary depending on your phase in life. So the key to staying within your threshold is to be attentive while you eat. **Savour every bit of what you eat, slowly and mindfully, and you will naturally find your threshold. All you need to train yourself to do, is to be attentive to your stomach.**

Look at the process of eating. It's about you

picking up food with your hands and taking it towards your mouth and chewing on it, and then taking it further inwards into your stomach, from where it travels to your intestines. There the food is churned and whatever is useful is picked up and transported to the cells of the body and what is not is taken to the rectum and pushed out of the system. We all learnt this in school.

So, eating is a process of internalisation. If eating employs one of our sensory organs, the tongue, shouldn't the other senses support this essential process? We have five organs that decide the reactions of our five senses: the eyes, tongue, nose, ears and skin. Sight, taste, smell, hearing and touch. These are the tools we are meant to employ to understand and gain knowledge about ourselves. Instead we employ them to distract ourselves from doing just that. We use them all the time to focus on the external world. Eyes watch TV, ears listen to voices on the phone or a speaker, skin touches the fork, spoon, keyboard or remote control, and the tongue is distracted by the salty and sweet taste in the food. We remain numb to the other tastes in the food.

We have to learn to experience **mitahar**. What's that? Mitahar loosely translated means sweet food or diet. Mita: sweet and ahar: food, diet or meal. According to me, the real meaning of the word dieting is mitahar.

No, I am not saying that you should be eating desserts, pastries, chocolates and mithai. What I am saying is that eating should always lead to a 'sweet' feeling. In the manner in which you exclaim, 'Oh such a sweet boy' or 'Oh, that's so sweet'; which means that my experience with this boy, girl, or thing has been pleasant. Similarly we have to learn to eat only to a point where our experience with food is sweet or pleasant, and when our body still feels light and fresh.

To experience this 'sweetness' or mitahar we will need to employ all our senses: tongue, nose, eyes, ears and skin. So you can't enjoy your favourite serial or catch up with friends abroad while eating. Your eyes have to watch the colours of your meal: the green in the sabzi, the red in the fruit, the yellow in the dal, the light brown of the chapati. The nose must be tuned to the aroma of the food, the skin should feel the texture of the food (oops, can't use your spoon then), ears should listen to the silence you observe while eating, and the tongue should open up to all the tastes in the food. Our brain takes time to tell us that we've eaten enough. And by the time we get the signal, we have usually eaten beyond our capacity. Experiencing food slowly—the essence of mitahar—keeps us in touch with our brain and our body. And it means we'll automatically stop when we've reached the threshold.

Hey, it's really not half as complicated as it sounds. Ok, let's try again. Eyes watch the colours of food, nose smells the aroma of food, skin feels the texture of food through your fingers, ears listen to the silence and the tongue opens up to the various tastes in the meal. Not convinced?

Ok, remember the time when you started to learn how to drive. A smelly, *Rangeela* inspired, Aamir Khan-wannabe driver sat next to you in a khatara car with extra brakes and clutch. Then he said in 'English': 'Newton, press clutch, first gear mein dalo, dheere dheere accelerator dabao aur ab dheere dheere clutch chhodo'. Ah, you tried and tried but every time you let go of the clutch 'dheere dheere', either the engine would shut down or the car would race about five metres and come to a grinding halt. About 8 days at the most and you start driving the car like makhan. Leaving the clutch and pressing the accelerator seems like a no brainer now. But in the first week of driving class of course we all suffer self doubt and are in awe of people who change gears faster than they change their clothes. 'Ah, will I ever be able to drive like that? Go from third to second on a speed breaker?' But before you know you have left the so called good drivers behind. Now driving has become second nature to you. You can listen to loud music (it's illegal though), type an email on your Blackberry, touch up your makeup, and sip your coffee while driving. But in the early days, when you were still learning, even if the cell phone rang you felt nervous, right?

It's pretty much the same with mitahar. Initially you have to eat in isolation and focus all your senses just on eating. You need this because you have to experience mitahar, that sweet experience with food, and learn to stop at that. Pretty much like the way you learn to stop at the sweet noise your engine makes when it's purring, beyond which you don't press the accelerator and let go of the clutch. Then, the car runs nice and smooth.

Guidelines

Before eating:

- Switch off your phone, TV and computer.
- Wash your hands (use a soap).
- Serve yourself half of what you usually eat, on a nice, clean plate.
- Preferably adopt the crosslegged posture or sit at your usual dining place.

While eating:

- Drink a glass of water.
- Start eating (preferably with your hands) and eat slowly.
- Chew your food slowly and deliberately.
- Use the entire mouth and don't just chew from 1 side of your jaw.
- While you still have food in your mouth don't pick up the food from your plate (Keeping food ready in your hands or on your spoon means you are eating fast and will ultimately overeat.)
- Eat with all your senses and think about how the food is nourishing you from within.

- Now if you want to eat some more, serve yourself a second helping from the other half that's left. But don't eat it all.

After eating

- Don't be in a rush to get up and get going. Stay where you are for a few minutes.
- If you're clearing up yourself, pick up your plate and clean it with water before leaving it in the sink. (Food that dries up on the plate will sometimes stay on the plate even after washing, and can cause stomach discomfort at a later point.)

Babies and Mitahar

Babies always instinctively know the right amount to eat and when to stop. Not just that, their feeding times are like clockwork. Ask any mother of a newborn. Babies will always wake up at their regular times, whether at 2 am or 6 am. They never seem to miss their meal timing, no matter how inconvenient it gets for their mother. And once they have had the right amount, they won't take even a sip more. If the mother continues to hold her baby by her breast after feeding, the baby will start suckling, playing or biting, but will never drink a drop more than it requires. And a change in a baby's feeding times only signifies that it is ill or uncomfortable.

This is how you experience mitahar. It's a good idea to learn to do this alone for the first few days, till you get the hang of it. And once you do it over and over again, the body learns to do it like a reflex action. Like driving, this too is about practice and regular practice will take you towards perfection. So you will, in time, be able to stop at the mitahar point even while eating in places with loud music, or while putting your point across during lunch meetings, while chatting with a group of friends, while picking up your food with a fork, chopstick, spoon, etc and while staring at presentations, TV, laptop, etc. (I don't recommend eating in such situations though as this obviously amounts to abusing the art you have developed, and should be kept to a bare minimum).

Leaving food on your plate

We have all grown up believing that leaving food on our plate is bad manners and an insult to food itself. A lot of times we 'finish' food on the plate even if we are no longer interested in it and even after our stomach is full (crossing the overeating threshold yet again). Leaving food behind on your plate will not be an insult to the millions who go hungry every night (when you come from a poverty stricken country like India, this is another association attached to not eating all your food, along with that of bad manners and insulting food). Overstuffing your stomach has not helped the poor (it never will) and it definitely doesn't help you.

A fit person is more capable of bringing about a change in society. Feel strongly about millions who go hungry every night? Get yourself in shape and start investing time (not just money) in community projects. And yes, leave food on that plate if you don't need it. Follow the rules of mitahar, so serve yourself small quantities to start with.

The 5 basic rules to increase nutrient intake

Alright, point noted: we should be eating in silence and while enjoying our own company. Now the next question is, what should we be eating? I will answer that in the next chapter but before I do so here are **5 basic rules for increasing nutrient intake**. By nutrients I mean carbohydrates, proteins, fats, vitamins, minerals and of course water. Of these, carbs, protein and fats are called macro nutrients because our body needs them in higher amounts, and vitamins and minerals are called micro nutrients because they are needed in smaller amounts. Also, 70% of our body is water, so this is something that our body needs all the time.

1. Eat food that is prepared fresh. And consume it within 3 hours of cooking. That means you shouldn't be freezing any food for the next day. Don't deep freeze cooked food. I know for most of us who work regular hours, it is almost impossible to have fresh food for lunch. But you can stick to this rule for breakfast and dinner. And let's face it, most of us in India have maids who come home in the morning. We might as well use this luxury.
2. The smaller the number of people the food is prepared for, the better its nutrient level. More the people, the earlier you start to prepare the food, and the greater the quantity of food cooked, the more oil and heat you use. That's

why restaurant food can never be compared to home food. And that's why, instead of picking up a salad from your favourite salad bar, you should take a tomato and cucumber with you and eat it as your own on the go salad.

3. Eat your vegetables and fruits whole instead of cutting them into pieces, because you lose vitamins from their surface. The larger the exposed area, the more the loss of nutrients. So eat a full apple, pear or plum, etc, and don't chop it into pieces. If it's a big fruit like melon or papaya which you simply have to cut, carve it into big pieces instead of pieces that you eat with your fork. So, hold the big piece in your hand and chew on it and literally let the juices flow. Messy but oh so satisfying. In the case of vegetables, don't store them cut. Never ever buy the pre-packed cut vegetables and fruits in the supermarkets. It's like buying food that's gone to rot. What's more, you're wasting all the packaging which comes along. (And please don't kill fruits in a juicer or mixer and pulp them into a juice. Not even if you retain the fibre. See box on fruit juices.)

4. Remain loyal to your genes and eat what you have been eating since childhood. If you are a Punjabi eat your paratha, as a Tamilian eat your idli, etc. Right from the time you're in your mother's womb, your body is used to eating, digesting and assimilating certain

foods. Almost everyone except a Punjabi will complain of a bad stomach after chole. There are two reasons for this: a) non Punjabis don't cook chole as well and b) they lack enzymes required for breaking down chole. Most of us now eat food of all kinds, it's being part of our global village. But try and eat at least one meal daily that reflects your own genes. My editor is Bengali and has grown up on her maacher jhol and bhaat. Yet now she lives in Delhi and eats north Indian khana. I've told her she has to try and have more fish and rice because that's what her genes know and love.

5. As much as possible, eat local produce and seasonal food. Climate, altitude, humidity, wind, soil quality, etc influence our digestive system and foods that grow locally. Ayurveda recommends tweaking your diet, habits and lifestyle according to the ritu, or season. Kareena ate momos in Ladakh and they helped her lose weight because Ladakh is dry, windy, cold and at an altitude of 3500 metres. If she ate the same momos in aamchi Mumbai which is humid, hot, and at sea level, she would have become fat. Mangoes are great in the summer. Eat them just once a day as a mini meal in themselves, and they will give you a season's supply of antioxidants. Store them in your fundu fridge for rains and you won't enjoy them as much; they won't taste half as good and would have lost most of their nutrients.

And the 6th rule—a calm state of mind

Real life example: My yoga mate, Prema (Stephanie is her 'mundane' name, she's an investment banker from Paris) and I decided to make a pilgrimage to Gangotri in the Himalaya, after our 2 week long Sadhana intensive course at the Sivananda Ashram in Netala, near Uttarkashi. For 2 weeks, we had spent almost 9 hours daily in intense yoga practices, and had led a very disciplined life at the ashram.

As both of us drove towards Gangotri, about 100 kilometres away from the ashram, we stopped at Harsil, 30 kilometres before Gangotri. Now Harsil is considered to be *the* most beautiful valley in the Indian Himalaya and is one of my all time favourite places. As we made arrangements for a night's stay, breaking journey, we chanced upon one of the thousands of apple trees that grew in Harsil. It was the end of September, so the trees were in full bloom. The apple tree was full of ripe and red fruit, and covered with deep green leaves. It stood by a refreshing, bubbly stream, against the clear blue skies and snow-capped peaks of the Himalaya. I saw women sitting under the trees cutting apples and drying them to make chutney. 'Do you sell apples?' I asked one of them. She nodded yes. 'How much?' 'Twenty rupees for one kilo,' she demanded. We were so happy that they were selling apples that we bought a kilo each. One of the women washed 2 apples in the stream and gave them to us to eat (complimentary, as we had bought 2 kilos).

I dug my teeth into the apple... ooh, ahh... It was

so crisp and so juicy, and it melted in my mouth. I felt something run down my elbow, and as I opened my eyes to see what it was (I had never eaten an apple so lush that its juice trickles down till the elbow) I saw Prema's face. Her face wore the same expression of bliss that mine was probably wearing. If there is God then we had experienced God in that apple.

After some time, Prema managed to break the silence. We promised each other that if we experience anything like this, we would let each other know, no matter where we were. I know in my heart that this was an experience of a lifetime. Chances of experiencing something even remotely similar are, well, remote!

I bet both of us absorbed every nutrient that the apple had to offer. We had followed all the basic rules to improve nutrient absorption. Also we had eaten with all our senses. The apple we held in our hand; we smelled its delicious, apply fragrance; heard the crisp sound it made as our teeth dug into it; saw the ripe, red colour of it; and of course our tongues tasted its sweetness. It was bliss.

Other than following the 5 basic rules of improving nutrient intake and eating with all 5 senses there was another major factor which led to our blissful experience: our state of mind. For 2 weeks we had been cut off from the rest of the world. We had stayed at an ashram by the Bhagirathi (that's what Ganga is called before she meets Alaknanda at Devprayag), led an exceptionally disciplined life, woken up early, slept early, practiced yoga daily, read spiritual books as a part of the course, did karma yoga (selfless work) and ate very fresh locally grown food with little or no spices. So, just fresh out of the ashram our state of mind was at its calmest.

A calm state of mind actually helps us to absorb all nutrients from the food we eat. Boring? **Ok how's this: a calm state of mind actually prevents conversion of food to fat.** Now that's interesting, right? When your state of mind is calm and composed, you secrete the right amount of digestive juices. Which means that you are now ready to take in your food, break it down, digest and assimilate it. This is when your food reaches deep inside you, to all the tissues and cells which need energy.

When the mind is stressed, agitated, worked up, sad, angry and distracted you don't secrete any digestive juices. You sure eat, but nothing gets digested or absorbed. Because you are feeling disturbed or stressed in your mind (which the body perceives as a threat to its survival), most of the food gets converted to fat (the natural reaction of the body when it thinks it's under threat). Stress (caused by work, finance, relationships, traffic, lack of sleep, etc) leads to the secretion of cortisol in our body. The function of cortisol is to lower our metabolic rate, prevent fat burning and help convert food to fat. The body has learnt this response as a means of fighting drought, famine, floods, etc. It also led to the evolution and survival of the human species from the caveman or cavewoman mode to what we are today. The body can't fathom why we get stressed over petty things like deadlines, break ups, home loans, debts, what to wear, etc, but decides nevertheless that if we are stressed it's a risk to our survival—and goes all out to protect itself. The means of protection is making us fatter. So the cells which need energy remain deprived, and the already big fat cell gets bigger. Now you are not eating your food, your food is eating you!

But we can reduce our cortisol production by leading disciplined lives. Waking up close to sunrise, exercising daily, finding means of self expression, and by keeping all our senses focussed on one thing at a time. (This, of course, is the ideal. In my last chapter, I write how we can incorporate these ideals into our daily lives). This is especially true of eating. So while eating, if you want a calm state of mind you can't afford to dissipate your energies. All your senses should be focussed on one thing: food. That way you will eat your food (and food won't eat you); and you will secrete your digestive juices, nutrients will be delivered to cells which need energy and won't get converted to fat.

Agni and digestion

Your agni or digestive fire needs to burn nice and bright. When this fire is active and strong you can digest and assimilate all the nutrients from the food you eat and not just that—the fire also helps you get rid of the toxins from the food.

How bright our agni burns depends on our state of mind. When you are trekking in the Indian Himalaya, you could be carrying all the cash in the world, but all that you can buy as you go from one camp to another is a hot cup of chai (only if you are lucky). But of course on your long trek you share biscuits, chocolates, etc with your trekking mates. Then, on reaching the camp you eat everything in sight: pakoras, parathas and the works.

Compare this to your NY holiday. You walked all day and shopped (on 5th Avenue, of course). Shopped till you dropped and then ate, carefully but ate nevertheless. (Come on, shopping is tiring plus you were on a holiday and it's NY. You just have to walk so much!)

So when you come back home from NY, you discover you have gained weight (not again) and the clothes that you bought no longer fit you. When you come back from the trek in Himalaya, the clothes don't fit you either but that's because your size has dropped.

You walk in NY and you walked in the Himalaya. You ate a lot in NY and in the Himalaya. The difference of course was in the state of mind. While cities and shopping pulls our senses in all directions, mountains, rivers, trees, skies, pull the senses inwards and make us feel more centred. So, when the senses are calmed the fire burns brighter and yes, it also burns more fat this way.

Nutrient to calorie ratio: why a paneer paratha is always better than a pizza

We need calories to lead a healthy and fulfilling life. The most important thing that eating does is provide us with calories or energy. When a baby is delivered and the umbilical chord is cut, the first thing she does (after crying) is consume calories by drinking her mother's milk. Consuming calories is one of our first acts upon our birth. So let's quit counting calories. What we need to worry about (if at all) is whether we are maintaining a good nutrient to calorie ratio. Simply put, it means that every calorie we consume should be loaded with nutrients.

'Kitna calories?' is the most irrelevant question for somebody who is trying to achieve a lean body and better fitness levels. (The second most irrelevant question is 'How many calories am I spending?' Third: 'What's my weight?' Fourth: 'What's the serving size?'). Calories ko maro goli. Really.

Unfortunately our perverted minds have come up with a way of consuming way too many calories without getting our nutrients. So we process our foods to the extent that it kills all the potent nutrients in them, robs them off all the fibre (which adds bulk to food: ever noticed how you can barely eat a few mouthfuls of brown rice while white rice you can stuff like no tomorrow?), reduces the vitamin and mineral content and literally leaves them empty. This emptiness is then filled with trans fats, emulsifiers, preservatives, salts, sugars, the works. (Nowadays even instant noodles come fortified with 'calcium, iron, protein'. Please give us a break. It's the equivalent of raping a woman and then marrying her to justify the rape.)

Preparing your body for fats

If you have a wedding, party, Christmas or Diwali feast or anything else coming up where you simply must eat that pudding, modak, laddoo, jalebi or special mithai, what do you do? Declare that you are on a diet and deprive yourself of the yummy mithai and desserts? Or fake a tummy upset? Worse still just not turn up for the party? No, too boring. Instead all you have to do is tell your best friend, your body, that you will be eating more than usual for Diwali, Christmas, Eid, your anniversary or party, etc. Your body likes being taken into confidence (who doesn't), and it responds to this communication by increasing your metabolic rate, secreting more digestive juices, enzymes, and sending more blood flow to your stomach. So now your mind and body are both prepared for the onslaught of food and the calories that come with it. Because you have not fooled your body into believing that you will not be eating, and then loaded or stuffed your mouth last minute (completely catching the body unaware and disrupting its normal metabolism), your body will reward you by not storing the excess calories as fat. Remember the section on food and stress? You will convert maximum food to fat when you're disturbed in any way. So dig your teeth into that luscious pastry or gulab jamun. Enjoy it and eat it guilt free. **A relaxed state of mind is the best preparation for any indulgence.**

Make sure that the food you eat is not 'empty' and processed; that it's natural and full of goodness like paneer, cheese, peanuts, nuts, milk, yogurt and whole grains. Let me elaborate a bit. Let's say that you have a choice between 'fattening' peanuts and low fat protein enriched or fibre added biscuits. What do you choose? If you believe that marriage justifies the rape, then the biscuit by all means. Otherwise pick the peanuts. Your peanuts with 'good fatty acids' will not just increase your HDL or good cholesterol and protect your heart, but also the protein, vitamin B3, folic acid, fibre, amino acids like arginine and high levels of antioxidants in them will leave your skin looking fresh, aid digestion, and provide you with longlasting energy. So for all the calories you have consumed, you have also collected nutrients: the experience is enriching and not emptying. While the fibre and protein enriched biscuits give you nothing.

Here's another example. Happy to eat pizza with low fat cheese or normal fat cheese but avoid paneer parathas? Paneer paratha is way richer in nutrients, fibre, antioxidants, essential amino acids, essential fatty acids, minerals like calcium, etc. So maybe eating a paneer paratha is equal to eating 2 to 3 slices of pizza, in terms of calories. But compare the nutrients. A pizza is 'empty', darling.

Another of my favourite examples is that peculiar practice where people avoid coconut chutney with their idli or dosa, or avoid kela chips fried in coconut oil and go for the low fat or no trans fat chips. Now why are you avoiding the chutney while eating south Indian food? The coconut in the chutney adds fat to the carbohydrate rich idli or dosa, thereby actually lowering its glycemic index and the rate at which it gets converted to fat. Additionally, coconut is rich in MCT or medium chain triglycerides, which help effect digestion and improve metabolism. MCT are used as fat loss and endurance building supplements because they are readily burned as energy and not stored as fat. So eat your idli with the chutney. And deep fry the banana chips in coconut oil. Choose these chips over the loaded-with-preservatives and MSG chips available in the market. Ideally, of course, I would never recommend anyone eating deep-fried food regularly, but at least with the kela chips your fat comes with other goods. **Bottom line: when it comes to food think nutrients, not calories.**

Once our fundas are in the right place, that is 'the 5 basic rules of nutrient absorption', all 5 senses are employed for eating and state of mind is calm, we can talk about carbs, proteins and fat (in the next chapter).

Cheat sheet

- The key to eating right is to focus while you eat: switch off the TV and mobile phone.
- You can digest the most amount of food between 7 am and 10 am.
- Stress can make you fat.
- Last night's sabzi and dal retain very little nutrition the day after.
- Think global eat local; eat dosas in Chennai, momos in Ladakh and pasta in Italy.
- Stay close to your genes: as much as possible eat the food you and your family have grown up eating.
- Tell your body when you're about to indulge and it will help you deal with the extra fat you're going to be eating.
- It's better for you to have a paneer paratha than a pizza. How many nutrients a food has is much more important than how many calories.

3

What to eat: rethink

We now know how to eat. Now the next question is what we should be eating. Everybody seems to know what we should not eat (sweets, fried food, etc) but there is confusion about what we should eat. Let me try and answer them here.

All about carbs

Carbohydrates are responsible for providing our body with the energy it needs for normal day to day functioning. Additionally, they play many other important roles:

Carbs
1. Synthesise and form our DNA and RNA
2. Synthesise hormones and fatty acids such as cholesterol
3. Generate powerful antioxidants and protect our cells from damage and ageing
4. Cleanse the body
5. Help hormone and immune functions
6. Regularise bowel movement because of their fibre content

Most importantly, carbohydrates help in the functioning of our brain cells and neurons. **The body is able to carry out its functioning without carbohydrates but it cannot *think* without carbs.** We have all experienced this. If we are hungry or haven't eaten for a long time, we get edgy and irritable, and generally lose our sense of reasoning and judgement.

Carbohydrates are found in all plant foods like fruits, vegetables, grains, legumes, etc and in milk and milk products. (They are absent in meat and meat products). Carbohydrates are classified as simple and complex, we all know that. Now what we also need to understand is that carbohydrates are also classified by their glycemic index (GI) and glycemic load (GL).

The glycemic index ranks carbohydrates depending on how quickly they lead to an increase in our blood glucose and insulin levels. High GI or 'fast' carbs lead to a quick sharp rise in the blood glucose levels and low GI or 'slow' carbs lead to a slow, steady rise in blood glucose levels. **High GI foods (fast carbs) get converted to fat quickly and low GI foods (slow carbs) have a much better chance of getting utilised for energy instead of getting stored as fat.**

Glycemic load is based on glycemic index and portion size. It is achieved by multiplying glycemic index by the carb content of a particular food and dividing that number by 100. So the glycemic load of a particular meal is the sum of all glycemic loads of all foods consumed during the meal. What this means is that even if you fill up on a lot of low GI food, its effect on your body will be similar to eating a small portion of high GI food.

There is a lot of talk about no carb and low carbs, but is it really advisable to cut down on carbs? Well, no, not if you are Indian. Indian diets have always been high in carbohydrates. If you search the web you will find wealth of information on glycemic index and load. But does all this information help us achieve our goal of adopting a healthier lifestyle and staying fit? Instead I have often seen people getting, what I call, 'diet diarrhoea'. They get so much of conflicting and confusing information that they can digest and assimilate nothing. In the end everything that they have read is lost or wasted. What stays is a drained out state of mind. And they are still not able to decide if they should eat carbs or cut carbs.

That's exactly why this book is going to focus on using common sense (according to Anil Ambani, the most uncommon thing in this world). Carbohydrate provides our body with many essential nutrients and fibre. Fibre slows down the release of sugar in the blood stream and reduces the glycemic index of food. Fibre also leads to a feeling of fullness, and helps in digestion and bowel movement.

Choosing the right carbs

Ok, so what point am I trying to make? If you care about your health eat your carbs. Carbohydrates, other than performing all the functions listed above and the ones that you studied in biology class, help you burn fat. **In fact, in the absence of carbs, fat cannot be utilised for energy.** Now we all want to burn fat, right? So put that roti, rice, dosa, idli, poha, upma or paratha back on your plate.

Just be careful to choose slow carbs. Carbs that retain their fibre are low on GI; so if you look at brown rice and white rice the main difference is in their fibre content. Brown rice contains all the fibre and that's why it has higher nutrient content and better fat loss properties. White rice on the other hand has lost all its fibre and nutrients thanks to the processing. So it's high on GI and low on fat burning properties. Other low GI foods are; jowar, barley, bajra, nachni, legumes, dals, wholewheat. All sweets, biscuits, pizzas, processed juices, sherbets, jams and jellies are high on GI because they have no fibre. It takes no time for our body to convert the sugar that comes from these foods to fat. Stick to low GI food as a general rule. **Your body can take high GI food only after exercise, when your body needs instant sugar.**

Now how do you use the information you have on glycemic load? If you eat a lot of brown rice, even if it is low on GI, the GL of your meal will go up because you will end up consuming lots of carbohydrates at one time. This will again convert food to fat because there will be too much sugar load at one particular time. So use your common sense. Just because it's good for you don't eat all you want; always keep in touch with your stomach and make sure you don't cross the overeating threshold.

Carbs and the freedom struggle

During the British rule where direct propaganda against the administration was not allowed, freedom fighters would go around spreading their message as spiritual leaders, dancers, drama troupe, singers, etc. My grandfather often sang me an old anti-Raj Marathi song every time I dipped my Marie biscuit in his tea (He had a song for everything: for waking up in the morning, bedtime, dealing with tantrums, dressing up, going for a function, doing homework.)—pav, biscuit, khanuni banala, banala daru baaz, parkiyaan chya latha katha nahi tumha laaj, naka naka naka ho sodo parvasta. Loosely translated in English (without Mr Raj Thackeray's permission) it means: You eat bread, biscuit and drink like the invaders [the British], they kick you but you have no shame, don't let go of your legacy and culture. The song is about how the British influenced the food that Indians ate and the grand style in which they introduced the biscuit to the Indian diet. Bread, biscuit and alcohol are all bad carbs or fast carbs and provided no nourishment to the Indian mind which then easily accepted slavery. (Processed food leads to dullness and lethargy). You really know that you have won over somebody when they start eating (and not yawning) like you. Today of course we all would like to move towards a 'sarhade he kyun?' state and like to think the way Farhan Akhtar (in 'Rock on') wants us to. But back then it was relevant and in Konkan this song touched many a heart.

The Atkins attitude and the South bitch

In the west, carbs are often eaten stripped of fibre: processed flour is used in their bread, cakes, pasta, pizza, etc. The western diet usually lacks that great Indian concept of dal-sabzi (both of which add fibre), as part of our every meal. Vegetables come, if at all, mostly in the form of salads camouflaged with croutons and fattening dressings. So the slow or good carb content in their diet as well as fibre is negligible. Even cereals are mostly processed with added sugar. Atkins and South Beach diets, which promoted low carb, were such a huge hit because following them meant going off bagels, pizzas, pastas, muffins, etc—foods which don't provide the body with any nutrients. The sad part is that people lost weight but also their health. These diets so severely restricted carbs that it interfered with dieters' day to day functioning and thinking. In fact the 'Atkins attitude' is a well documented phenomenon. Low carb diets lead to depletion of serotonin, a neurotransmitter in the brain responsible for feeling of well being, happiness, and satisfaction. Atkins attitude makes your moods go south (as in bad). South Beach diet also rhymes with south 'bitch' (which is what happens to women who are on it). So irritability, restlessness, depression, anxiety are common especially if you are a woman, because you have hormones which can wreak havoc when set off balance by a low carb diet. Worst of all, you go through the whole circus but the weight comes right back and that too, double of what you lost. All that you lose at the end of this big diet drama is your confidence and self worth.

To overcome the Atkins attitude, nutritionists

recommend complex or slow carbs, very much prevalent in the Indian diet. (Mind you, Indians abroad totally eat the Indian way. Food and its wonderful associations help create the Pind in Calgary, Surat in New Jersey, Ahmedabad in Queens, and Cochin in Oman). But all the google ranis and rajas of mera bharat mahan (women or men who depend on google for all information and entertainment they need in life, one google window always open, searching desperately for something they must know) blindly copied the low carb diet fad of the west, but instead of looking like a Hollywood star (that's what low carbs promised, you see) they ended up looking like deflated pizzas. Use your common sense, don't get off carbs. Especially with the meals you eat at home, where you use chakki atta and eat hot breakfast daily. Carbs help you burn fat, keep your bowels clean, reduce bloating and aids metabolism (because they also provide the all important vitamin B responsible for converting food to energy.)

In India, or for Indians anywhere, avoiding carbs need not be high on the agenda. Look at Indian foods: poha, upma, parathas, idlis, dosas, dhokla, rice, dal, roti, sabzi, rajma, chole, etc. Most of our carbohydrates aren't processed, and they retain their fibre, vitamin B and minerals. Also, if you look at our cooking style, everything gets a tadka or seasoning of 1 to 2 teaspoons of oil with some seeds like mustard, jeera (which add fibre, vitamins, minerals and essential fatty acids), etc. The addition of a fat like oil or ghee in the tadka lowers the

GI. The primary foods that we use in India, our cooking methods and our food combinations all work at reducing glycemic index and increasing fibre content of food.

Now if we are also eating the Indian way, that is sitting on a mat, on the floor, using the crosslegged or sukhasan posture, saying our prayers (India is multicultural and religious, and all religions recommend prayer before eating) where we offer our food to God and consume the rest as prasad or God's blessing, then we will remain super duper lean and fit.

So eat high fibre carbohydrates as much as possible and cut the biscuits, cakes, pastries, pizzas and anything that's low fibre. At the end of this section I have a list of carbs that you shouldn't worry about, and a list of carbs that you should ideally eliminate or reduce from your diet.

I can't emphasise enough on the importance of 'Eat local, think global'. Punjabis in the great land of Punjab only have aloo parathas for breakfast and not dinner unlike the people of Mumbai, Delhi, or Bengaluru (where parathas are blamed for putting on weight). Also, south Indians who eat rice eat the unpolished variety which retains most of the bran or fibre and B vitamins. Once in the cities, its white polished rice, so white it can put your rock to shame.

Type 2 diabetes

Indians are prone to diabetes. This is a consequence of insulin resistance. Insulin resistance is caused by consuming too many unhealthy or fast carbs, in addition to stress, obesity and inactivity. This condition can be managed very easily by reducing the glycemic load at one time; ie eating small portions many times a day and consuming slow or low GI carbs.

The pancreas plays an important role in food digestion, secreting enzymes that break down fat, starch and proteins in the small intestine. The beta cells of the pancreas produce insulin and alpha produce glucagon. When there is a rise in blood sugar level the beta cells secrete insulin, which stimulates cells in the body to grab glucose, leading to a fall in glucose levels. It also instructs the liver to store glucose as glycogen (glucose reserve). When glucose levels fall below a set point or optimal level, the alpha cells secrete glucagons, which instruct the liver to convert glycogen back to glucose. These two pancreatic hormones are responsible for maintaining healthy blood glucose levels. Consumption of high GI or processed carbs leads to a sharp increase in blood glucose levels in a short time period, followed by a huge dip in its levels; which overburdens these two sensitive hormones and leads to obesity, especially around the stomach. Over a period of time, these hormones lose their sensitivity to blood glucose levels; this is called insulin insensitivity, or stress induced or type 2 diabetes.

Damage control: have your gulab jamun and eat it too

Sweets and desserts are high on the glycemic index because they are high in everything that is processed; sugar and flour. So should you avoid them completely? A lot of clients ask me this question before embarking on their diet plans: 'So does this mean that we will never be able to have our brownies, gulab jamuns, pizzas, burgers?' Here is the answer: you can safely eat your brownie, gulab jamun, etc without getting fat. Two things: eat them not more than once a week (and that's the most you're allowed!) and don't eat them with a meal. A brownie or dessert after a lavish dinner means pucca conversion to fat because glycemic index and load are both high. But if you want to have the gulab jamun with all the sweet juice and have developed the discipline to eat just one, then eat it by itself as an in between meal. This way, the high glycemic index will be set off by low glycemic load (less food at one time) and this will improve the chances of your body not converting the sweet treat to fat. (There is a good chance there is no conversion to fat, in fact.) So eat your pizza, but stop at one piece. **Where the glycemic index is very high, reduce the load.** As I have mentioned, the best time to eat high GI food is post exercise.

When to eat fruits

We should eat fruits when we are in a fasting state or when our liver store is empty: so, first thing in the morning on an empty stomach, or immediately after physical exercise. Any time aside from this, the body converts the fructose from the fruits into triglycerides (as explained earlier in chapter 1). This is why I am not a fan of fruit juices. Not only does fruit juice give you four to five times the amount of fructose you get in one serving of a fruit, it also lacks the goodness of the fruit's fibre. So eat your fruit first thing in the morning—but before your breakfast, not with it.

Alcohol

Alcohol is treated as foreign substance by the body. This is the first thing to remember, rather than how many calories it has (which by the way is double than that of carbohydrates at 7 calories per gram). So when we drink any kind of alcohol, the body immediately puts its fat burning on hold, and starts to metabolise the alcohol; to get rid of this foreign substance. Thus, the body isn't just ingesting a higher calorie substance, it's also giving up its fat burning, at the same time. The other thing to remember is that alcohol leads to an increase in estrogen in the body. So you will see drunk men do typically 'girly' things like getting emotional, crying, giggling and talking loudly. This is also what leads to a 'beer belly'. Women naturally have more fat on their stomachs because this is where the foetus grows, as nature intended; and estrogen replicates this in men. Interestingly, estrogen is also one of the reasons why women can't usually drink as much alcohol as men. Now are you still going to have that drink tonight?

If you are, then make sure that you eat something before you do. Food will act as a buffer and limit the damage. Also for every glass/peg/serving of alcohol have at least 2 glasses of water. One more reason why alcohol is so dangerous is that it is extremely dehydrating. (seen well dressed men, unzip and have a go at the wall of your fav night club? Or women making their way in the loo with their bladders threatening to burst?) Drinking water will take fun out of drinking, complain most of my clients. Well, but at least it will safeguard you against damage. So if you must drink, drink no more than once a week, and always after food (or with it but never on an empty stomach) and with at least a glass of water. Hello, beer and wine are alcohol too, so treat them with the same gravity that you treat whisky, rum, vodka, etc.

Carbs you should never eat (these are high GI and zero on nutrient)	And how to cheat on them
1. Biscuit	Eat them when you've done a very long physical activity like trekking, 2 or more hours of walking or shopping. In day to day life, restrict to one a week! I think biscuits are more harmful than cakes and pastries because no one worries about scarfing them down.
2. Cakes and pastries	If you can't bear to give up your favourite chocolate pastry, you're in for good news. Have it first thing in the morning. Don't replace your nutritious meal with this but have it in addition to it. Croissant lovers go ahead as well. But don't indulge yourself more than once or twice a month.
3. Pizza	One slice (we're talking fast food pizza) and as a meal by itself. Perfect for after a long boring meeting.
4. Drink syrups, cold drinks (all drinks made from these, including sherbets, etc)	After being out in the sun for a long while; the sugar will have less of an effect. Also after a long day or if you're on holiday, have one every 2 to 3 days.

5. Mithais and all desserts (chocolates, etc included)	Eat as a meal by itself. Have your mithai either an hour and a half after your lunch, or first thing in the morning. Again not more than once a month, if you have to have it!
6. Deep-fried food like samosas, pakoras, vada, bhujiya and kachori	Eat first thing in the morning. Halve your first meal and have your deep-fried goody along with it, or as a meal by itself later in the afternoon. But restrict yourself to only one of these. And do not eat a mithai with it. You can have one of these treats once a week, but again only if you're eating correctly all seven days and working out at least three hours a week.
7. Sugar	2 teaspoons a day max. Most of you have this in your tea or coffee, so bear this in mind...
8. Alcohol	With a meal or after a meal. Never on an empty stomach and never have anything deep-fried with it.

Carbs to eat through the day that ensure optimum fat burning and sustained release of blood sugar (these are low GI foods):	Carbs to be consumed after exercise or any stressful activity (high GI foods):
Phulkas or rotis made from gehu or wholewheat atta, jowar, bajra and nachni/ragi. Also idli, dosa, uttapam, appam, neer dosa, upma, brown rice, wholewheat bread, oats, barley, semolina/rawa/suji, vegetable parathas, koki, homemade khakra, dhokla, iddada, besan or mung dal dosa, chillas, sweet potatoes, unripe banana, all lentils.	Boiled potato All fruits White rice and dal White bread sandwiches or toast Fruit juices Homemade ladoos
How to eat them	**How to eat them**
With vegetables and in small quantities. They can be part of your breakfast, lunch and an evening meal by 5:30-6 pm.	Within ten minutes of your workout. I don't usually recommend fruit juices but this is a safe time to have it. As for rice and dal, for anyone who works out at home, this could be an option depending on when you workout. You can also eat fruits first thing in the morning.

All about proteins

The word protein comes from the Greek word 'proteios' which means primary. It has many roles to play in our body without which normal functioning can be impaired. Some of these functions are:

1. Making antibodies, which are our primary defence system against infections.
2. Movement and muscle contraction, which we get from contractile proteins (without which we could do little).
3. Catalysing metabolic and biochemical reactions through enzymes. Enzymes take part in all chemical reactions in the body. Example: enzymes helps the digestive system in breaking down food.
4. Picking up signals from the body and sending them to a cell that needs it; hormonal proteins work as messenger proteins (like insulin).
5. Making up cells and tissues; structural proteins such as keratin, collagen and elastin do this important job for us, creating connective tissue, tendons, ligaments (responsible for keeping hair, skin, nails healthy).
6. Help transport nutrients from one part of the body to another; the haemoglobin does this.

The primary function of protein is to build and repair your body. In fact amino acids, which are the building blocks of protein, are what make up all the different parts of our body. There are about 20 odd amino acids, which can be compared to alphabets. Different amino acids come together and make specific proteins that go into creating hair, nerves, or the matrix of the bone, cartilage, hormones, enzymes, etc. Much like the combination of different alphabets make words. They are also responsible for all types of physiological processes such as generating energy, recovering from illnesses, maintaining our bodies and their growth, fat loss and even mood and brain function. Amino acids are divided into two major categories: indispensible amino acids (IAA) and dispensable amino acids (DAA). As their name suggests, indispensible amino acids need to be provided by the body through your diet and can't be made by the body. DAA, on the other hand, can be manufactured by the body, so it's not so necessary to provide them through diet or food.

Protein, like carbohydrates, is your ally when it comes to getting a lean, toned body.

First it helps you burn fat. To lose fat the body must be able to increase the circulation and mobilisation of stored fat. Then these fats need to be converted to energy (commonly called fat burning). To improve circulation of stored fats and to break it down into energy, the body needs several nutrients. One of the most important nutrients it needs is methionine, an IAA. Methionine can be supplied to the body in adequate amounts by eating a well balanced diet and by consuming good quality protein like fish, eggs, milk products, whey. A diet which restricts protein will lack methionine and will not facilitate fat burning.

Second, it's absolutely vital for anyone doing physical activity. During any form of exercise, the body and specifically our muscles go through microscopic wear and tear. Loss of muscle tissue or its breakdown is associated with ageing and the **one thing that will turn exercise into an anti ageing activity is protein.** Why? Because amino acids help us repair our tissues and recover from the stress that exercise places on our body. Post exercise the body is in need of some fast carbs (the only time that the body needs high glycemic index carbohydrate is post exercise) and a quick supply of amino acids. The fast carbohydrates lead to a spike in the insulin levels of the body. The cells in the body then pick up the glucose and amino acids that they need for quick recovery from strenuous workouts. Without protein, working out is fruitless. No wonder people who exercise but don't watch their diets ultimately deduce that exercise doesn't work for them. Because without the amino acids reaching sites of action, exercise really doesn't work. Fat and carbohydrate can both provide us with energy but cannot do the repair and recovery work that protein does for us. **I would go to the extent of saying that if you can't arrange for your post workout meal to have protein and high GI carb, you are better off not working out.** Just like if you don't have money for petrol you are better off not driving.

What doesn't work — high protein diets

In recent years, there has been a protein craze in the dieting world. People who want to lose weight swear by high protein diets. Good old chapati and rice has practically been shown the door, and egg white and chicken are ruling the roost. But at what cost?

Real life example:
  'Hi, listen it's just been 4 days and I have lost 1 kilo. Can this be true? Are you a magician or what? I am eating so much, my god! How could I have lost weight? I don't even have any pressure on my head ya. I am just not feeling like I am on a

diet. I am not feeling helpless, angry, and irritable. Rujuta, is this going the way we want it to be? I am feeling very happy. Should I feel happy? Because happy is not what I feel when I am on a diet.'

Email at 7am from one of my 'I hope I am not wasting my money with you and I hope you know what you are doing' client.

I spent 2½ hrs with Ami, instead of the usual 1½, for the first consultation. (Prachi, my assistant, was very upset with me for running over by a whole hour. She could bring herself to forgive me only because it was the last appointment for the day). Now throughout our consultation, Ami only expressed displeasure over the food I wanted her to eat. Her basic problem was that this plan just didn't seem like a diet. Ami had recently shifted from London to Ghatkopar (central suburb of Mumbai, packed with rich Gujjus).

'Please understand, I want to lose weight', she pleaded with me. 'And I am spending a lot of money on you.' (Gujju. Very Gujju!) 'I will look like my daughter's stuffed toy after this, I want to look like Barbie.' 'Then eat', I reasoned with her. 'If not eating would make you look like Barbie, you would look like her by this time. But clearly its not going to.' Ami had a super will power, she had done it all (in terms of diet). The one that had showed her maximum 'results' was where she went on a 'shake diet'. She had subsisted on some expensive protein shake for breakfast, lunch and dinner. And that was it. Other than that she had eaten nothing.

She lost weight, yes. And did she gain it all back, sorry double of all that weight, and that too in half time? Yes, of course, because that's the only pattern that these so called diets follow.

Ami had a problem that her breakfast had dhokla and lunch had phulka, sabzi, kadhi, etc. 'I just need a high protein diet. Actually, I know so much about diets that I can put myself on one anytime. I have put so many of my friends on diet and they have lost weight also', she said. Ami, for her part, was 30 kilos more than what she had been just 10 years ago. In her thirties now, an early marriage, settling in a foreign country and child birth had all contributed to her weight gain. 'Look I know Kareena Kapoor keeps saying that she eats paratha for breakfast, normal sabzi, dal, roti, pasta, etc, but I am not stupid to believe that. Size zero aisa kaise hoga? I wanted to meet you to understand that what is this diet all about. Reality mein kya hai?'

'Ami, seriously, you are going to lose weight only if you eat. Eating nothing se kya hota hai tumne experience kiya hai. Why don't you give your body a chance to eat healthy and to eat what it enjoys eating?' Finally and reluctantly she decided to 'try this also'. Needless to say, she was overjoyed to find that she had lost 1 kilo in 4 days, and that too 'by eating'. Nothing short of a miracle for Ami, nothing more than a natural consequence of eating correctly for me.

Ami and my art promoter (from the first chapter) both did their versions of high protein diets. But why does it not work?

Now for protein to work as it is supposed to (growth, repair, maintenance, gene expression, etc), the body should get its supply of carbohydrate and fat. Without these nutrients, protein is wasted. So called high protein diets only replace your carbohydrate and fat sources with protein rich foods. This in no way ensures that you are reaching your daily requirement of protein. And in case you are reaching your daily requirement of protein, then in the absence of carbs and fat it will be rendered useless. **When too much of protein is consumed at one time, it doesn't get stacked away for future use, instead it is converted to fat by a process called deamination.** It will just load the liver where it will get broken down to glucose. So your expensive and difficult to digest protein (yeah, chicken, fish, egg white are tough on your system) is getting used for energy. Something that a banana could have easily done. (Cheap on your pocket and easy on your digestive system.)

Learn to be shanaa with your protein. Whatever source you choose, veg, non-veg or a supplement, know that without a balanced base line diet, protein by itself will only lead to irritability, sleeplessness, constipation, mood swings, and muscle catabolism or wasting. Will it lead to weight loss? Yes, it will. When the body is given only protein and very little or no carbohydrate, the body first gets rid of its glycogen stores (glucose or sugar stored in liver and muscle) and loses water. After that, it actually attacks the muscle tissue itself, burning the amino acids for energy. The result is muscle catabolism and lean mass loss. Accordingly, regular exercise and a smart use of carbohydrates in the diet lead to protein sparing. What this means is that protein is not burned for energy instead it is used for its intended purpose.

What doesn't work either — low protein diets

At the other end are people so paranoid about protein that they feel it should be avoided at all costs.

Real life example:
My clients never disappoint me with their diet histories. So at one such meeting, Kedar sat down with me and related to me his diet tales. He didn't look overweight and had a passion for eating healthy. 'Madam, please remember, pure vegetarian. Any fruit, any vegetable, any soup, no problem, I will eat whatever you tell me.' His cholesterol levels were up and he had come to me because one of his friends who had had high uric acid levels had recommended me. 'Accha, tell me why you gave him protein? And how come his levels came down after eating protein? Raaz kya hai madam? Kuch goli dete ho ke mantar phukte ho?'

'Tell me your story Kedar,' I demanded.

'Accha, see I eat 1 kilo of fruits in the morning. Only 1 cereal, jowar for lunch with green sabzi and then soup, salad, fruit for dinner. And to cleanse my system I take lime shots.' 'What's that?' I asked. 'Arre, 15 to 16 nimbu squeeze karne ka aur peene ka. Kya cleanse hota hai total system. Arre aisa pata chalta hai ke sab saaf ho raha hai andar se.' After this, from upbeat he started slipping into the sad mode. 'Abhi kya hai, weight lose to kar diya (20 kilos) but my cholesterol levels have gone up. I hear so many stories, heart attack ka. Abhi kya hai you see, I am approaching forty, my business is very good, so no tension, family ka tension to chalta rehta hai par kuch serious nahi, but yeh weight lose karne ke baad cholesterol kaise badha kya pata?'

'Kedar, pehle tum apna raaz batao. Mantar padhke nikalte ho saara din? How can you survive only on fruits?' I asked.

'Arre, I am a fruitarian. When I first went on the diet for 2 months I had nothing but fruits. Tabhi to weight lose hua. Wajan to hatana padta hai madam, aap ko to pata hoga? After that, last month se mere naturopath/nutritionist (he swore by her) ne ek jowar roti chalu kiya. Very high in iron, aap ko to pata hoga.'

'Nahi yeh sab mujhe nahi malum,' I told him.

'Joking na?' he said, surprised.

'No, serious. Yeh majak nahi hai Kedar. Iron, kya iron? Iron absorb karne ke liye aur usko haemoglobin mein banane ke liye body ke paas kuch chaiye ke nahi?'

'Haan isliye to 1 kilo fruit madam.'

Kedar's story was not new to me. Nor was his enthusiasm to follow what he believed was a 'natural diet'. He was 20 kilos overweight before his diet. Now with no protein in the diet, the weight had crashed. His self esteem should have soared (he is totally the bindaas types), instead he started feeling 'Something is not right'. He met me because he couldn't figure it out. Why it was that people asked him 'Bimaar ho gaye the kya?' instead of 'Wah, kya Aamir/Shahrukh jaise lag rahe ho.'

'But my favourite, madam, is Saif in *Race*. Sachi, aap ko aisa lagega ke aap ka client hai isliye, lekin usne jo *Race* mein style mara hai... [eyes lighting up with mix of admiration and respect] Wah! Nawab style ekdum. Anil Kapoor ko to kha dala. Matlab maine to Bipasha ko bhi nahi dekha, sachi.'

'Aap bolo abhi mere diet se achha aur kuch ho sakta hai? Fruit, sabzi—no oil, and soup. Perfect. Phir bhi yeh problem. Aisa ki, mota tha—to no problem. Now weight lose—but cholesterol problem. Kya kare aadmi bolo?'

You know what I am getting at. No protein but only carbs, that too in restricted amounts. And yes, some fibre. But protein and fat being completely avoided. Instead nimbu shots to 'cleanse' the liver, kidney, etc. I guess the only thing it cleanses completely is the brain. So let's not bore you with what all could have possibly gone wrong, which led to Kedar's ageing (from looking like 30 he started to look 38), his cholesterol going up and haemoglobin levels going down (which led to the entry of 'iron rich' only-one-jowar roti at lunchtime).

Kedar's diet is not only restricted in fat but also

in protein. When we are deprived of a nutrient like protein, weight loss occurs only because the body breaks down its muscle to make up for the resultant lack of amino acids. Your lipid profile, your cholesterol and triglyceride levels, can go up because in the absence of a primary nutrient like protein, the body experiences stress. Also, haemoglobin is not just iron but iron (heam) + protein (globin). In a protein and calorie deprived state, to think that jowar will lead to iron absorption and normal haemoglobin levels, is foolish to put it mildly; in a calorie deprived state, the body has no nutrients to make any haemoglobins.

When I explained all this to Kedar, he looked like a shattered man. 'Matlab yeh sab mehnat karke mein to chutiya ban gaya! Sorry madam.'

'Its ok, Kedar. I can understand how you feel.'

'Par sab rishi muni to yahi khate the na?' he said, referring to his fruit only diet. 'Yes Kedar, par tum rishi muni ho kya? Tum share bazaar mein paisa lagate ho. Tum jungle mein rehke, dhyan dharana to nahi kar rahe? You lifestyle is different, right?'

'Haan, woh to hai. Sirf Lakhsmi ji ki karta hun, subeh nikalne se pehle. You should also have madam, Lakshmiji, sitting posture not standing. Nahi to kya, chanchal hai na, nikal jaati hai.'

Ok, so I now planned Kedar's diet for him. Again the same issue, 'Itna khaunga to patla kaise rahunga?'

'Kedar, nahi khaoge to rahoge kya, pehle socho? Cholesterol badha hai, triglyceride bhi badh sakta hai. [It was already border line.] Woh badha to diabetes bhi ho sakta hai. Ek ke baad ek. Tumko kya karne ka hai bolo? Young dikhne ka hai? Baal sar pe chaaiye? To pehla body ko kuch karo. Usme thoda investment karo. Nutrition daalna padega. Asli grahasthapak ke tarah khao, rishi-muni ke tarah nahi.'

'Haan, yeh sahi baat hai madam. After all I am a family man.'

In my opinion, lots of preconceived notions about dieting—that it will leave dark circles under your eyes, give you chipped nails, hair loss, frustration and anger—are linked to protein deficiency. Amino acids are necessary for normal hair growth and lustre, strong nails and smooth skin. Without them not just how you look, but how much fat you burn, will be affected.

Sadly when it comes to eating correct, there are no shortcuts. High protein or low protein, both diets fail to improve health and body composition (reduction in fat and increase in lean body weight). Improving health and increasing our sense of well being is the basic premise of 'going on' a diet. The safest thing to do with protein is to tread the middle ground. That is, consume an adequate protein diet and eat a diet with balanced amounts of carbohydrate and fat so that protein is free to perform its primary functions. **Our protein requirement stands roughly at 1 gram per kilo of body weight.** So if you are a 60 kilo individual you will need 60 grams of protein a day. Most of us don't get our quota of protein, and a professional dietician is the only person who can really assess if we're getting enough.

Protein requirement varies at different stages in your life. Young and adolescent children, pregnant and nursing women, aging and/or stressed individuals actually need more than this stipulated 1 gram per kilo of body weight. Regular exercise, frequent travel, etc also increases the protein requirement of the body. The body wastes about 40% protein in just few days of experiencing mental stress, surgery, prolonged sickness and starvation. During these times not just protein but even the total calories consumed need to go up. When your protein intake is adequate you will feel strong, sleep well and look great.

If you do follow the four principles, and increase your nutrient to calorie ratio, you should be okay. However if you're working out and travelling a lot, I would recommend you go on a protein supplement.

Choosing the right proteins

Protein is found in all meat, fish, egg, legumes, milk and milk products and soy. It is also found in minute quantities in all your other food. Whey protein, a powdered milk product (see box in following pages), has the best biological value and can be used to meet your daily requirement of protein; or to supplement protein in your diet. Importantly, legumes like dal, rajma, chole are not just a good source of protein but they also provide essential carbs and fibre.

Though non-vegetarian sources tend to contain higher amounts of protein (in terms of both quantity and quality, because they have both the IAA and DAA), they are also usually high in fat (especially saturated or bad fats) and lack fibre. **It is for this reason that I ask my clients to avoid red meat (too much of saturated fats) or at least restrict it to no more than once a week.** And while eating red meat we must take care to choose the leanest of cuts, with all the skin and fat removed.

All other forms of protein can be eaten daily. Fish and eggs are better than chicken; fish scores the highest marks because it's a rich source of omega -3 fatty acids. But remember: all the non-vegetarian protein options are tough on your body and hard to digest. Soy is great. But because it can increase estrogen levels (the female hormone in your body) it should not be overdone. If you like your soy, eat one soy product a day but not more.

Some vegetarians depend almost entirely on soy for their protein intake. Not a very good idea. It is always a good idea to eat from a variety of sources of protein, because of each source's different kinds of amino acid content. Vegetarians should always eat food combinations because most vegetarian sources have limited amino acids. So the amino acid that your roti lacks is provided by dal, or the one that your rice lacks is provided by kadhi (made out

Whey protein

Whey protein has got more bad press than whisky, gin, rum, wine, beer, and even grass. Whey protein is a powder made from milk which you mix with water to turn into a drink. It has the best biological value of protein; which means that almost every gram of whey you consume gets used for its intended purpose and is absorbed by the body. Whey isolate, made from whey protein is a boon for lactose intolerant vegetarians like me as it doesn't irritate the stomach or the intestines.

Whey protein has been accused of affecting the kidney, liver and heart but this isn't true. Although superstars, cricketers and doctors advertise for the so called 'Protein drinks', (especially for children, easy targets perhaps, not to mention their parents' obsession with their height), the reality is that these drinks are so loaded in sugar and have such miniscule amounts of protein (not to mention poor biological value too) that they really do much more harm than any good. And a nutrient is never specifically beneficial for a particular age group. Whey protein on the other hand is easy on the system, has zero sugar, and is easy to digest. If you weight train regularly or run long distances, whey protein will become a necessity. (It also comes in all flavours: chocolate, vanilla, strawberry and many more.)

Word of caution: whey protein is a supplement. It is not supposed to be used as an alternative to eating correctly. Consuming adequate protein, carbs and fat by means of a well-balanced diet is a must. Only then can whey protein be of any help. Like with everything else, if you overdo it or depend on it alone to provide you with protein, you stand to lose out on its considerable benefits.

of curd), or the ones that certain vegetables lack is provided by seeds like jeera and til that we use in our Indian cooking. As I mentioned earlier, what is important in protein is the amino acid content, especially the IAA content. There are eight IAAs and we should have all of these IAAs in our main meals. This is easier for non-vegetarians. However, choosing a variety of foods throughout the day will ensure that we don't fall short of IAAs. So vegetarians too can get all their IAAs, if they ensure that they eat a variety of foods throughout the day.

How to eat your proteins

How much of the protein we eat is actually reaching the sites it is meant to and how much of it is being used for its intended purpose is determined by:

- Total calorie value of your meal: if you are short of your quota of calories, the protein you consume will be used to create energy and will not do its repair work.
- Method of cooking: most proteins need to be cooked well as it makes it easier on your stomach. This applies to all meats, egg and pulses. Only fish and dairy products can be eaten raw. Undercooked protein is a disaster. Protein needs a certain amount of processing. Ever eaten undercooked chicken breast, rajma or chawal? I rest my case.
- And most importantly your state of mind. So even if Sonu and Monu eat the same grams of protein of the exact same amino acid profile, how well their body utilises this protein (whether its chicken breast or rajma chawal)

will vary. Sonu exercises regularly (expect his organs especially intestines to be strong and healthy), doesn't watch TV or chat on phone while eating, has his meal well cooked and is in the company of his girlfriend while eating, doing some romantic gup-shup. Monu doesn't believe in exercise (weak stomach and digestion capacity) and is having a fight over the phone while eating his half there-half not there meal. Who will absorb protein better? Sonu! Full marks to you. Of course this rule applies to all food, but particularly to protein as it's the toughest nutrient to digest.

Veg vs non-veg

I can't talk about proteins without touching upon the veg versus non-veg debate. This eternal debate is about much more than complete and incomplete proteins, but it does deserve special attention with regards to protein.

So which is better, veg or non-veg? A lot of people take immense pride in being vegetarians. The idea behind vegetarianism is that of ahimsa, non violence or compassion towards all. So when you order your veggie Mac with Coke, veggie delight pizza with Pepsi, puri, bhaji, shrikhand, chole batura, dal bhatti, jalebi, churma, rasgulla, etc is there no himsa there? You are killing your own stomach. Too much food is a form of cruelty too; you are being cruel to your own stomach.

Maybe you cringe at the sight of chickens packed in stuffy carriers and goats on altars, and can't generally stand the idea of a chicken or non-veg dish on the same table as yours; or despise people who eat non-veg. But are you being truly compassionate? Or is your compassion reserved only for animals? (No offence Ms Maneka Gandhi.)

Contd. There is enough evidence to show that the human digestive system is better suited for vegetarian food. Moreover, vegetarian eating is said to reduce world food problems. (And even global warming. Livestock CO_2 emissions are rapidly adding to the global warming phenomenon.) But what we need to understand is that veg or non-veg, what we eat is a matter of personal choice.

Vegetarians (including me, I am one by birth and by choice) need to understand that being a vegetarian is about practising non violence and compassion towards all, including yourself. Ahimsa is a much deeper philosophy (it made MK Gandhi into a mahatma, and caught the entire nation's imagination), and not as superficial as ordering eggless pastry, or disallowing non-veg restaurants in your neighbourhood or forcing all restaurants in the neighbourhood to serve only veg food. And like everything else this ahimsa has to start with being kind or compassionate towards yourself. If we continue to load our stomachs then all benefits of vegetarianism are lost. A stuffed stomach is in a much more pitiful condition than the chicken in the stuffy carriers going over speed breakers.

On the other hand there are non-vegetarians who can't stop pitying the poor ghas-phoos eating vegetarians. They argue that vegetarians are deprived of meat which is so rich in proteins and great in taste. But tell me how much of protein can your body assimilate when you stuff chicken biryani like there is no tomorrow or eat mutton and chicken in every form, size and shape at 3 am in the morning at Bade-miyaan after getting sloshed in the night with all the clubbing.

Again, our body's ability to digest and absorb proteins depends on our state of mind, time of the day and most importantly on how full we are feeling. So if you have dabaoed on your favourite chicken dish thinking its all protein so it won't convert to fat, you are just being hopelessly optimistic.

Veg or non-veg, whatever you choose to eat, be kind to yourself and your stomach and eat only a little at one time. Remember the golden rule, just fill half your stomach at one time. With this you will be practising ahimsa even while consuming non-veg food.

The reality is that proteins can be assimilated by vegetarians and by non-vegetarians only if they eat with all their senses, follow the 5 basic rules of improving nutrient intake and never overload their stomachs.

Proteins you should never eat...(these are high on saturated fats)	And how to cheat on them
1. Sausages 2. Cold cuts and processed meats 3. Beef 4. Lamb 5. Pork	Eat them as your first meal or after your post-workout meal. Eat them once a week provided you follow the four principles and exercise three hours a week.
Proteins to eat through the day, that ensures optimum fat burning and sustained release of blood sugar	**Proteins to be consumed after exercise or any stressful activity**
Eggs, chicken, fish, all milk products (paneer, cheese, yoghurt, milk), soy milk, tofu, sprouts, lentils, nuts	Protein powder (providing at least 20 grams of good quality protein per serving or 4-5 egg whites and this is a must)
How to eat them	**How to eat them**
With vegetables, carbs or by themslves. Eggs, lentils, dairy products, soy and fish can be eaten at any time. Chicken should be eaten at the end of your working day as it's relatively tougher to digest and can slow your body down during your working hours. The hours between 6 and 8 pm are a good time to eat fish and chicken as the body needs these nutrients then to repair itself.	Eat them within ten minutes of your workout.

All about fats

'Look at me, from everywhere I am perfect. I just need to lose this', she said picking up flab from just above her low waist jeans and then pointing to the 'saddle bags' which bulged from under her butt, just at the top of her thighs. 'So many of us can empathise with what Radhika is saying,' Mahesh her husband said. 'My only problem is this,' pointing to his pot belly. 'I am also perfect, otherwise'.

See we all are perfect just the way we are. But we are too occupied doing too many imperfect things. Just one of them is banning fats from our diet. Fat plays a big role in our body. Most importantly, it helps us survive during periods of prolonged mental and physical stresses, sickness, and prolonged starvation. Fat is stored as adipose tissue in the body from where energy can be used in these extreme cases. It's due to this ability that the human species has evolved and survived. So fat is our body's answer for bad times. It is the only nutrient that can help us survive through the toughest phases of our life. Thus your so-called lean times will actually make you fat. Corollary: fat or good times will make you lean. **So eat fat to lose fat.**

Fat is energy dense substance providing us with 9 calories per gram. Carbs and proteins provide only 4 calories per gram. Other than survival, fat also performs the following functions in our body.

1. Transports vitamin A, E, K, D, which are also known as fat soluble vitamins
2. Protects vital organs like heart, kidney, liver, lungs, etc
3. Acts as an insulator and prevents loss of body heat
4. Is a part of the protective sheath covering the nerves and helps in nerve transmission
5. Stimulates flow of bile and emptying of gall bladder
6. Required for milk production and the normal growth of a foetus in pregnant women
7. Makes up much of the brain (more than 60% of the brain is composed of fat), and helps it function smoothly
8. Lubricates joints

In short fat is required not just for optimum health but for the sustenance of life itself.

Now, there are many types of fat, each one having a specific role to play in the body. These fats can be roughly divided into the following categories:

Saturated fats

These are solid at room temperature: butter, animal fats (especially red meat), milk and milk products, coconut and palm oil. Long chain fatty acids are found in animal fats. These damage cardiovascular health and are hard to digest. Ghee (which is basically clarified butter obtained after milk is taken through a process of curdling and heating, or clarifying) has short chain fatty acids. These are easy to digest and promote good health. As a general rule, the fats in animal fats are tough on the body, while the ones found in dairy products are easily absorbed.

Anti-ageing

To keep the face and body from ageing, work at keeping body weight to optimum. Don't get complacent and tell yourself that if you were 65 kilos at 25, you can be 80 kilos at 40 years. No, not if you want a 'young' face. To have a young face, you have to reduce the gravitational force which is acting upon it; which simply means that you must not allow your body weight to go up from its optimum (and this is usually the one that you maintain in the prime of youth, at 18 to 25 years of age).

The second thing that you must do is include healthy fats in your diet, like nuts (including peanuts), cheese, ghee, paneer and fish. Including fats not just provides your facial skin with the moisture and raw material that it needs to keep from wrinkling, but also helps you to burn fat effectively there, by not allowing your body fat levels (body weight) to go up. Nothing keeps age off your face like fat (the right amount of it of course; the amount which keeps your body weight at optimum). The appearance of wrinkles and loss of suppleness actually has to do with loss of fat from the face.

Unsaturated fats

These are fats which are liquid at room temperature; so all oils except for coconut oil. Just like proteins have essential amino acids or IAA, which cannot be synthesised by the body and need to be provided by our diet, fat too has EFA or essential fatty acids. It's important to get them through our diet to maintain optimum health. Unsaturated fats are further divided into three groups.

Mono Unsaturated Fatty Acids (MUFA)

These are found in peanuts, olives, avocados, almonds. They are considered very crucial in maintaining the health of the heart. The popularity of olive oil has grown tremendously in the last few years, as has people's sense of how healthy it is. Indians, especially in cities, are switching to olive oil (extra virgin mind you) because it is being hailed as the saviour (our love for everything phoren). So, you're wondering as you're reading this, is it bad? No. But closer to home, **peanut oil (it's always been around) and that new entrant, rice bran oil, have a strong content of MUFA. Their fatty acid content is similar to olive oil, and they have a flavour which is much better suited to Indian cooking than olive oil.** Oleic acid (a component of MUFA) is great for moisturising skin, and to keep it glowing; some hair growth vitamins are made with it.

Poly Unsaturated Fatty Acids (PUFA)

These come in two types: omega 3 and omega 6. Omega 6 is found in sunflower, safflower (kardi) and soy bean oils (most vegetable oils are predominantly PUFA). Omega 3 is found in flax seed, walnuts and the oils in fish. Polyunsaturated fats have heart protecting values too. We should have equal amounts of omega 3 and omega 6. But in diets today, the ratio of Omega 6 to Omega 3 has grown as skewed as 20:1, which can lead to the hardening of arteries and an increase in cardiovascular diseases.

Trans fats
This is the new kind of fat which was created to preserve food and give it texture. It is made by converting unsaturated fats into saturated fats, by a process called hydrogenation. Trans fats are commonly used by restaurants, fast food chains and companies that produce food on a large scale and for commercial purposes, as it is cheaper. Most processed foods, store-bought cakes, biscuits and fast food such as pizzas, burgers and fries, etc have this kind of fat. It is rightly called bad fat as it increases the levels of low density lipo-protein or bad cholesterol in our body. This is the kind of fat that is best avoided.

Whichever fad diet you went 'on' you got 'off' it as quickly. Our poor body suffered, a silent victim of this abuse and all that it could do was endlessly yo–yo down from one weight and up to another. Like Radhika, all we ended up doing is get obssessed even more about the flab on our body. Hit it, wiggle it, abuse it ('yeh, yeh mera problem area hai'. Just look at us calling the part which has taken the maximum abuse a problem area!) and hide it, of course. Almost everything other than actually providing it with love and nourishment:

the only long term and effective solution to your 'problem area'. When you go on a crash diet or don't provide your body essential fatty acids through your diet, the system perceives stress and responds by storing more fat for you. And you can't blame your body. It is only activating its survival mechanisms and protecting you from any harm that may come with stress; preventing fat burning to try to improve your chances of survival, and lowering your metabolic rate.

Of course there are some smart marketing professionals who have gotten fat bank accounts on this 'kabhi on kabhi off' relationship. Enter low fat biscuits, low fat butters (height of hypocrisy and stupidity), low fat chocolates, low fat chips, low fat chaklis, low fat cheese, low fat ice cream, low fat everything. And how people flocked to buy them. 'I don't eat wafers, just these baked or low fat chips.' 'Not the normal ice cream but the low fat variety.' A lot of so called 'low fat' is a waste of money. You spend ridiculously high amounts to buy low fat cheese and butter which only has about 1 or max 2 grams of fat less than the regular 'full fat' variety. Low fat ice creams are loaded with sugar or sweeteners. Low fat chips are high in salt, and instead of being fried they are baked, as they proudly proclaim; which, however, requires just as much or only marginally less fat, as compared to deep frying. Above all, this is not the worst of it. Sadly, it is these low fat and baked varieties (everything that is processed) that contain the worst fat: trans fat. Trans fats are responsible for the hardening of arteries, increasing body fat, and causing many other health problems (obesity related conditions like insulin insensitivity, heart trouble, BP, joint aches, etc).

Real life example: Visible and invisible fat
'I am very careful about what I eat. I don't know why I am getting fat. I married into a Marwari family so you know how they are. [Referring to Marwari-in-laws in general.] They want desi ghee in everything. They can drink ghee. [True, I have seen this.] But because we stay on our own, I have good control over the kitchen. I have never given Mahesh any ghee on his rotis, dals or anything. He likes farsan for snacks in the evening but we only eat all low fat biscuits, baked chaklis, low fat chips, etc. Yet both of us are fat. What to do?'

Radhika was a very adventurous and compulsive dieter. She had gone on a '21 days-21 Marie biscuits a day diet' just months after her delivery. She had achieved 'terrific results': 7 kilos lost in 21 days! This time round, she said she lacked the required will power. 'Thank God you don't have the "will power",' I exclaimed.

Radhika, like a lot of us, had bought into the marketing gimmick of 'low fat', what is technically called 'invisible fat'. Which means that when you pick up the chakli, biscuit or chips, you don't see the fat in them so you are led to believe that they will not get converted to fat. In the homemade deep-fried chakli or pakora, or in the ghee on roti, you can see the oil in the kadhai and on the food item: this is called visible fat. So we think, 'I am eating fat, it will get converted to fat.' The truth is, however, that foods with invisible fat are full of the bad fat, trans fat, which is responsible for causing heart attacks, insulin insensitivity, etc. When fat is invisible you also end up eating bigger sizes, increasing the glycemic load and therefore your chances of getting fat.

How to eat fat

For a lean, toned body, healthy heart, supple skin and lustrous hair, make fat a part of every meal—or at least of three main meals. It's not just enough to eat food cooked in oil. Include nuts, cheese, or any other dairy product in your diet. Consuming healthy fats in healthy (read adequate) amounts will actually ensure proper functioning of the body and optimum fat burning. Fats, when eaten in combination with carbs and protein, work at reducing the glycemic index (refer to the section on carbs, earlier in this chapter) of food. So they actually work at slowly releasing sugar in the blood. This leads to effective fat burning, stable blood sugar, minimised hunger, a good mood and a glowing complexion.

So of course use oil as a cooking medium for vegetables and dal, as most Indians do; don't try to cut it out. **Preferably different kinds of oil. So if you cooked lunch in peanut oil, try soy or**

safflower oil for dinner. Include peanuts and cheese in your diet. They can often make up a mini meal by themselves.

Including fats in our diet is also known to reduce mood swings and depression. Children who don't get enough omega-3 can develop learning disorders. Is your girlfriend giving you grief when she PMSes? Just buy her a flax seed supplement or gift her a monthly supply of nuts.

Deep-frying

Limit deep-fried stuff but don't avoid it completely. Eat hot, homemade pakoras, bhajiyas, puris, etc. Deep-fried but homemade food is good for you. The oil is not reused (reusing oil oxidises the fat and makes it toxic), and the soda and excess salt is missing (both lead to bloating and gas trouble). Just make sure that you eat immediately upon frying. And don't remove the oil on these snacks using tissue paper or napkins, as many do. As long as you eat only 7 to 8 pakoras or 3 to 4 puris and this only once a month, it's really ok. Your body can take it. But the reverse is not true; that you can eat deep-fried goods frequently and in greater amounts (more than 7 to 8 pakoras or 3 to 4 puris), so you need to remove excess oil. No, you will get fat no matter how much oil you 'remove'. So just take the excess frying episode out. Fry, but only once a month.

Italians and olive oil

Olive oil is replacing good old shingdana oil, ghee and other traditionally used fats or oils in the Indian household. We now have Italian marble on the floor, their slick modular kitchens and yeah their olive oil as well.

That we are experimenting with all kinds of cuisine is great. But let's not forget that in embracing all this diversity, we shouldn't try to be exactly like the Italians or anybody else for that matter; although studies show that olive oil has amazing heart-protecting properties, let's not be quick to jump on the bandwagon. Look at the picture in totality.

The Padmanabham temple in Kerala has a sleeping Vishnu. No matter where in the temple you stand, you can never see the Vishnu (representing reality) completely. You only see him in parts. So in this world where Maya is at play we only see a part of reality and never the complete truth. First, let's remember that the above mentioned studies were based on Italian subjects. The health of the Italian heart is not just due to olive oil, but also due to many other factors. Their diets are also rich in fruit and greens (high in fibre), and they are accustomed to regular homemade meals (mothers dominate their children and rule over the communal family dinner table). Of course, there is also their wonderful, easygoing attitude, and generally more relaxed way of life. As I have always said, you need a good, relaxed state of mind for the heart to actually work well, and to enjoy good health.

In India we start at 9 am and work till 8 or 9 pm. We get little or no exercise, don't walk around our crowded neighbourhoods much, live in polluted cities, eat loads of processed foods, etc, but hey if we eat olive oil shouldn't it protect us? No, it won't. Our way of life is quite different. If you must emulate the Italians then you must emulate in totality, not just pick up a part of their lifestyle that is convenient. (Actually we do have some things in common: we both have mama's boys and possessive or pain in the neck mothers-in-law, but these are anything but good for the heart.)

118

Fat as an integral part of diet

Have you heard of Spiti? For the uninitiated, yes, it's in India. Spiti is a cold, scenic trans-Himalayan region in Himachal Pradesh which lies between Ladakh and Tibet. Going there is like going back hundred years in time. The area is totally Buddhist and thankfully untouched by the 'development' of the outside world. But don't get me wrong, they have good road networks, schools, electricity in every village. So what if the smallest villages have only a couple of houses?

The people of Spiti have a diet rich in what they call joun (barley), which is full of fibre, low GI carbs, protein and essential vitamins and minerals like iron and calcium. In addition to this staple, their diet is dominated by ghee, milk and cheese, mostly made from cattle that every family owns. The cattle are like part of the family; they stay in the same house and keep the family warm during the harsh, -35 degree celsius winter. Cattle that are brought up with so much love and attention, grazing freely (from the best quality grass), are known to be healthier and therefore produce better milk. Cheese and ghee that you get from this milk is nutrient rich and potent. Ghee is a part of almost every local dish in Spiti, and it even finds its way to the top of your glass: decorated around the rim, like salt on a margarita glass. Ghee for these people, exposed to harsh weather and a rough life, works as an antiseptic, digestive, immunity enhancer, cartilage and joint lubricator, while protecting the heart and the body in general from sun damage.

Ghee is even offered to the gods and is known to bring the spiritual side of a person to the fore. It blesses the Marwari (traditionally from the hot, dry, arid climate of Rajasthan) with sharp business acumen, and the Spitian (from their cold, dry, harsh weather) with a strong, well networked cardiopulmonary system. (Most of Spiti is at a height of 4000 metres and above.)

Make sure you have at least 1 teaspoon of homemade ghee a day, and have it guilt free. Ghee shall bless thou too.

Marwaris

More than 60% of our brain is made of fat. So that derogatory term 'fathead' could actually be taken to refer to intelligence! Including omega-3 fatty acids in our diet such as flax seeds, beans, dairy products including ghee, vegetables, nuts and of course fish, improve our native intelligence. Marwaris are known to have sharp brains, especially a business acumen that everybody envies. You will find them at the top of their fields almost everywhere, at IITs and IIMs, as directors, scientists, accountants and obviously industrialists. Look at what they eat: ghee rich meals. Now, is there a link between the sharp acumen and the fat they consume?

Our brain is made up of fatty acid and Marwaris have always traditionally consumed the highest amount of ghee of all Indian communities. (It's another thing that most of them are also fat. But this is usually because of the lack of activity rather than the fat in their diet.) So don't move that fat out of your diet. Instead start getting the fat in your body moving and working!

Cooking ware and utensils

Phek do yeh kadhai, yeh frying pan? No! Please keep them in your kitchen. Using iron tavas and kadhais is a great way to improve the iron content of your food, and it's also a safe metal to use. So is stainless steel and glass. Using aluminium cookware is dangerous as the Al leaches from the pot or pan, makes its way into your food, and finally into your body. Once inside the body, aluminium will neutralise digestive enzymes, increase risk of ulcers and if present in excessive amounts, even lead to Alzheimer's disease. So get that iron pot, pan or tava back on your kitchen rack. (Using oil or ghee while making dosa, paratha, roti, sabzi or dal, etc improves the nutritional value of your food and also leads to a favourable GI of food. So don't obsess over going oil or ghee free.)

Another note on this. The size of your cooking ware should be decided according to the number of people you are cooking for. Just like an oversize dress is a misfit (irrespective of brand and style), so are oversized pots, pans or vessels. This helps you save energy (yes, just switching to CFL is not enough) and prevents loss of nutrients due to overheating.

Fats you should never eat. (these are trans fats)	And how to cheat on them
1. Fats you get from red and processed meat	Eat them as your first meal or after your post-workout meal. Eat these once a week, provided you follow the four key principles (see next chapter) and exercise 3 hours a week. Never combine a bad fat with a high GI food; say rice and meat, or biryani. All biryani lovers, save your feast for Eid!
2. Fat in deep-fried food (pakoras, samosas, bhujia, etc)	Eat first thing in the morning. Halve your first meal and have it along with this. Otherwise have as a meal by itself in the later afternoon, but restrict to only one. Do not eat a mithai with your snack! You can enjoy one of these, once a week, but only if you're eating correctly all six days and working out at least three hours a week. Don't reuse the oil once you have deep-fried with it. Tip: avoid deep-fried food at large parties, because they are usually deep-fried twice.

3. Mithai, especially those made of nuts	Eat as a meal by itself. Have it an hour and a half after your lunch. You could also have it first thing in the morning. But don't mix it with your regular food.
4. Biscuits	Eat them when you've done a very long, strenuous physical activity like trekking, 2 or more hours of shopping. In regular life, restrict to once a week!
5. Cakes and pastries	If you can't bear to give up your favourite chocolate pastry, you're in for good news. Have it first thing in the morning. Don't replace your nutritious meal with your pastry, but have it in addition to it. Croissant lovers go ahead. But don't indulge yourself more than once or twice a month.
6. Pizza	1 slice (we're talking fast food pizza) and as a meal by itself. Perfect for after a long boring meeting.

Fats to eat through the day, which ensure optimum fat burning and sustained release of blood sugar	Fats to be consumed after exercise or any stressful activity
Nuts, avocados, olives, milk and all milk products (cheese, paneer, ghee, yoghurt), oils used in cooking, coconut, flax seeds, fish	If you have issues losing body fat or a cholesterol problem, then make sure you have a fatty acid like flax seed or an omega-3 supplement.
How to eat them	**How to eat them**
Oils to prepare food, ghee as seasoning and the rest as meals by themselves. Make sure your quantities are right and that you eat 2 or 3 of these each day as part of your daily diet. If you feel dull after a main meal and are craving either sugar or coffee, have a fatty acid supplement, such as the omega-3 rich supplements, fish oil or flax seed, after it.	Eat them within 10 minutes of your workout.

All about vitamins and minerals

All vitamins and minerals play an extremely important role in our body as catalysts, co-enzymes (these help enzymes), and co-factors (these support chemical or metabolic reactions) of our metabolic reactions. Vitamins and minerals don't provide our body with any energy or calories but they are important so that we can use our energy or calories well.

A high intake of processed food, stress and other lifestyle factors like smoking, late nights and inactivity are increasing our need for vitamins and minerals, and reducing our ability to absorb them well. None of these nutrients can work in isolation. For calcium to do its work in the body it needs 24 other nutrients to be present, in the right amount and at the right time; while iron requires adequate amounts of protein as well as vitamins B and C to be at hand, to form haemoglobin. You will need a well-rounded diet, regular exercise and to be in a relaxed state, to improve the efficiency of vitamins and minerals.

Laloo Prasad Yadav, India's most hated and loved politician, said at the *Hindustan Times* Summit recently: 'Coalition ka zamana hai.' He could well be describing the way nutrients work in our body. Gone are the days when only one party or one vitamin, mineral or macro nutrient like carbs, proteins or fat ruled. Just like India has realised that the bigger parties need the help of smaller, unknown parties to create a central government, so should we realise that for fat loss and a lean body, the answer doesn't lie in majority or single party government (ie high protein, low carb or low fat diets) but instead in coalition raj. Vitamins, minerals, protein, carbs and fat all need to get adequate representation in our diet so that each one of them can carry out their specific functions to the best of their abilities; only then can we enjoy optimum health (just like that ideal stable government at the centre).

Vitamin A

Found in whole and low fat milk, dark leafy vegetables, all the orange, yellow vegetables and in the liver and kidney. Forms of vitamin A found in plant sources are called carotenes.

We need it because it supports our immune functions, helps improve eyesight, is crucial for the growth and development of our body, and is a potent antioxidant which protects cells against free radicals.

Take it when you're stressed, or travelling. One of the reasons why you get ill immediately after crash dieting or too much exercise or a period of stress is because of the deficiency of vitamin A. So if you have a stressed out lifestyle, you are going to need some extra vitamin A—and the best way to do this is to increase your carotene content. So get more green, yellow and red in your plate. The best time to take a supplement of vitamin A is after the most stressful period of the day, after a big workout or a long flight. Carotenes are also a good way of combating acne, and help prevent cancer, maintain a healthy reproductive system and reduce vaginal infections.

Vitamin D

Found in our body, which produces vitamin D upon exposure to sunlight. It is the sunlight vitamin. To get this vitamin, get your daily dose of sunlight. The best time to do this is around sunrise (the sun is not harsh or harmful for the skin at this time). People of north India have a favourite activity in the winters. It's called dhup sekna, or sun bath. It's a great way to get that daily dose of vitamin D, and of course to warm yourself up during the winters. Apart from this, we can also get vitamin D from fish and egg yolks. Plants are not such a good source of this particular vitamin, but green leafy vegetables are your best bet.

We need it because it aids calcium absorption. Bowing of legs, curving of spine, loss of bone density, joint pain and discomfort have to do with vitamin D deficiency. The elderly, especially those in nursing homes, are usually deficient in this vitamin because of their lack of sun exposure. It also has anti-carcinogenic properties, especially when it comes to breast and colon cancer. These forms of cancer are most common in places which don't get enough sunlight.

Vitamin E

Found in polyunsaturated vegetable oils like corn, soy, sunflower, safflower oil and seeds, nuts, whole grains. **Processing and overcooking foods drastically**

reduce vitamin E content. So when you make maida out of wholewheat or pulp your vegetables like you do in pav bhaji, there is almost no vitamin E left in them. Asparagus, green leafy vegetables, berries and tomatoes are good sources of this one.

We need it because it protects the heart, keeps the skin young, prevents nerve and muscular weakness and is a poweful oxidant.

Take it when you've eaten a lot of fried food, bakery products and consumed high amounts of fat. Fat gets broken down and damaged in our body by a process called oxidation; vitamin E prevents fat from turning toxic in our body. So if you ever consume bhujiya or pakoras, don't forget your E. Working out, sun exposure, viral infections and diabetes all increase the need for vitamin E consumption.

Vitamin K

Found in green leafy vegetables, green peas, green tea, oats, whole grain. It's the most neglected vitamin because vitamin K deficiencies are very rare.

We need it because it plays a major role in blood clotting, which is why it's a life saving vitamin. Recent studies have also shown that it is important in preventing and treating osteoporosis, and for building healthy bones. So, an important vitamin for women, who are more vulnerable to this disease.

Take it if you are suffering from excessive menstrual bleeding: excessive bleeding is often a sign of low vitamin K levels. Any vitamin supplement should give you more than your quota.

Vitamin C

Found in most fruits and vegetables. Most animals can make their own vitamin C: the human body however cannot. But the good news is that there is plenty of vitamin C in most of the food we eat. Vitamin B and C are water soluble (and hence they are also depleted as our body loses water), so our body needs a fresh supply daily. **Vitamin C can be easily lost by something as simple as cutting fruits and vegetables. We lose it more when we keep them covered in a refrigerator.** So anything that increases exposure of fruits and vegetables can lead to almost 90% loss of vitamin C.

We need it because it is critical to our immunity, helps manufacture hormones, collagen, maintains our respiratory system and lung function and is a powerful antioxidant. Vitamin C also plays a role in protecting us against heart disease, has a supporting function of vitamin E in the body, and protects sperms from damage.

Take it as a regular supplement. It's vital if you're a smoker (both active and passive), have a hectic social life and are dealing with a lot of stress.

Vitamin B

These are many vitamins clubbed together: thiamin (B1), riboflavin (B2), niacin (B3), pantothenic acid (B5), pyridoxine (B6), biotin (B7), folic acid (B9) and cobalamin (B12), all make up what we call vitamin B or B complex.

Found in fresh fruits, vegetables, whole grains, nuts, eggs, fish and cheese. Of these, B12 is found mostly in non-veg sources, so vegetarians have to take extra care to include this vitamin in their diet. Curd and cheese have good levels of B12, created through a fermentation process from milk (this fermentation increases B12 amounts).

We need it because it takes part in metabolic reactions, helps metabolise carbohydrates, aids digestion, improves nerve function and prevents depression.

Take it as a supplement at the start of your day with your breakfast so that you can utilise nutrients better throughout the day. PMS and bad moods can be prevented with a good supply of vitamin B just before your periods. Vitamin B counteracts Chinese restaurant syndrome (symptoms are mild headaches, bloating and sometimes nausea) which we get by eating MSG, found increasingly in processed foods. For lustrous hair and pink nails look to B for help.

Fibre

This is the one nutrient in your food which is essential not just to prevent constipation or regularise digestion, but also to prevent you from overeating. It is truly zero on calories, and just adds bulk to what you are eating.

Foods with fibre take longer to chew and thus our eating time increases. (The brain registers that it is full only after 20 minutes). This gives the body a chance to know that the stomach is full, and reduces our chances of overeating. As the fibre moves in our intestine it picks up wastes (almost like a jhadoo) and adds bulk to your stool (and not just your food). So, it makes going to the toilet a pleasurable experience too. And here, it will reduce the time spent in downloading!

It's clear that fibre has many benefits for all of us who want clear stomachs, glowing complexions, lean bodies and a good fitness level.

But don't be stupid and buy fibre added foods or add fibre to your atta, sabzi, buttermilk, etc. This mindless addition of fibre will come in the way of the absorbing of vital minerals like calcium and iron. Instead, focus on eating unprocessed wholesome foods which are naturally rich in fibre like brown rice, wholewheat, barley, raagi, jawar, bajra, chole, legumes, nuts. And cut down on the biscuits, white bread, burger, pizza or maida. And importantly: avoid overcooking sabzis and killing fruits and vegetables in the juicer.

Minerals

Calcium

Found in dairy products, tofu, green leafy vegetables, nuts, seeds and in fact almost all wholesome food. It is the most abundant mineral in the body.

We need it because it maintains the health of bones, joints and teeth, is responsible for all muscular contraction, for clotting of blood and to regulate blood pressure.

Take it as a supplement daily. Bone is a dynamic living tissue in the body, being broken down and rebuilt daily, even in adults. Thus, calcium is essential in maintaining good bone health on a daily basis. A diet that is high in processed foods, caffeine, alcohol, sugar and sodium reduces calcium absorption. So does regular intake of antacids and laxatives. Thus, here is one mineral we all must supplement in our diet. If you are using a calcium supplement, check what compound it uses. **A calcium citrate or lactate (soluble in form) compound is absorbed much better by the human body than the popular calcium carbonate or phosphate supplements.** Use a supplement of 1000 milligrams a day for optimum health.

Iron

Found in meat, fish and eggs (all non-veg sources). Veg sources are garden cress seeds (traditionally used to make laddoos for pregnant and nursing women), bajra, jowar, other whole grains, fresh vegetables and fruits. For iron to be absorbed effectively, we need adequate amounts of vitamin C and B (specifically B12) in our body.

We need it because it is a part of haemoglobin which transports oxygen from lungs to different tissues of the body and carbon dioxide from different tissues to the lungs.

Don't take iron supplements. Just like in case of calcium, processed foods, caffeine, anti depressants, sodium, sugar (including desserts, mithai and chocolates that we eat because of PMS) reduce absorption of iron in the body. The best strategy to improve iron intake is not to take iron supplements, but instead to create an environment in the body which will encourage iron absorption. Reduce your intake of sweets and caffeine, and increase vitamins C and B, in addition to drinking adequate amounts of water. Deficiency of iron is common especially in women. During menstrual periods women lose blood (good blood and not impurities, unlike what we believed earlier), and with it we lose important minerals like iron, copper, magnesium, etc.

Selenium, zinc, chromium, magnesium, manganese, copper

Found in fish, egg, whole grains, fresh veggies.

These minerals are gaining importance, not just because they are essential to preventing diseases but also because they are antioxidants, and promote fat burning in our body. Insulin insensitivity is a common reason for gaining fat and is rampant in urban India and in the west, and these minerals have proved to be efficient in improving insulin sensitivity.

Zinc and chromium are of paramount importance for good skin and hair growth, and to prevent acne and wrinkles. Zinc also plays a role in normal testosterone function and aiding muscle growth. For protection against free radicals, selenium is vital. Additionally, copper is required for optimum iron absorption; while manganese is responsible for thyroid function and blood sugar control. Magnesium helps lower blood pressure, eases PMS symptoms and lowers LDL levels.

These are just the main vitamins and minerals; there are many like boron, molybdenum, iodine, potassium and inositol choline that I don't really mention in this book. But does that mean that they are less important than the ones I have mentioned? Not at all. Nor are the many vitamins and minerals that are still undiscovered.

Supplements

In an ideal world, we wouldn't need any supplements; our food would supply us with all the vitamins and minerals we need. But we don't live in an ideal world, do we? Our soil is contaminated; our fruits are covered with pesticides and injected with glucose, polished with wax. And what's worse, our crop is transported in trucks for long distances, where it loses the little nutrients it has while waiting for 3 days for octroi clearance to cross to another state. Then, of course, the way that we store our grains, fruits and vegetables at our big malls is disgusting. (Good only on the display, but not in the warehouse which have poor storing conditions, not to mention pests, etc.) Even once the food is in our kitchen, when we cook it, how we store it, our state of mind or our cook's state of mind while cooking, the number of sauces, seasonings and other preservatives we add while cooking, and of course our state of mind while eating; all of this has made using supplements a necessity.

In an ideal world, you shouldn't be vying for a bigger house, bigger car, trophy husband or wife, and should be content with all that you have. Greed, anger, lust, hatred, jealousy shouldn't even touch you. You should be growing your own food, milking your own cow, waking up with the sunrise, sleeping just after sunset. If your life is like this, you won't need any supplements.

But it's more likely that this is what your life is like: thick curtains in the bedroom keep the sunlight away, air conditioning keeps you perfectly cool, a car and maybe driver takes care of transport; you eat takeaway for lunch, have little or no exercise, go clubbing at least once a week, engage in passive or active smoking regularly, do drinks at least once or twice every week and in addition to all this, have numerous worries—you want to shift to a bigger house, would like to make much more money than what you are making currently, etc. This is far from an ideal life, and what it means is that your body just isn't absorbing all the nutrients it needs. If you think that taking supplements is being unnatural, living like this, you are just being a hollow idiot.

What takes me by surprise is how people who regularly do joints (now that's herbal right?), are active only after 11 pm, have no clue of where their vegetables, fruits, grains, atta, etc is coming from, and are happy to pop a painkiller daily are so paranoid about the side effects of vitamin and mineral supplements. The lifestyle that they are leading is already bringing hordes of side effects upon them (some of which last a short time: headache, stomach ache, lethargy, irritability, and some which will last forever: heart attacks, insulin insensitivity, clogged arteries, depression, obesity, etc). Sometimes I suspect that they don't want the benefits of food supplements to wash away these side effects that they have spent a lifetime earning.

I know that vitamin and mineral supplements are no replacement to healthy eating, regular exercise and a positive attitude. But when you have a base line diet in place, workout regularly and are compassionate towards yourself and the world, food supplements will help make them work at their best.

Doctors don't recommend supplements—because they have little or no knowledge about them outside of what the marketing representative of a pharma company is willing to share (including kickbacks, nothing wrong with that of course). But any doctor worth his or her salt will admit that they have limited knowledge about supplements, mainly because they only studied nutrition briefly. Most of them may have done one paper on the subject in their first year of medicine. After which it's goodbye to the science of nutrition. (Unless a doctor develops an interest in the subject and signs up for a course on nutrition science).

Look for information in the right place. With all due respect, doctors know as much about supplements as CAs, engineers, editors, etc; basically any other well-educated professional. Chances are your trainer, yoga teacher or massage therapist will know much more than them (because they are required to read up and update themselves in the field of nutrition). Doctors are sometimes asked, 'So, what's your opinion on this protein shake?' And an honest 'I don't know much about it' is taken as something against the protein shake. This is also because our mind already has a negative image about it. Even if the doctor had said something like 'Excuse me, I think I am getting a call', this would be taken as a negative verdict for the protein shake.

The field of nutraceuticals[1] is growing as a science. The supplements that we need on a regular basis are vitamins like A, E, B and C, and minerals like selenium, zinc, chromium and calcium. I really don't understand the logic behind taking a daily vitamin E after a heart attack or a daily calcium tablet after a fracture. They should be taken as preventive strategies. If they are good for recovery, they are even better before the damage, to maintain good health.

The stress that we experience is a major reason for nutrient depletion in our diet, and so is urban living. By 2050, much of India will be urban, say many news reports.

In 2003, I visited Ukimath, a small hamlet just off the Rishikesh-Kedarnath highway. The GMVN

---

1 Extracts of foods claimed to have a medicinal effect on human health, usually made available in capsule, tablet or powder form.

guesthouse there has only two huts (a representation of the tourist flow) and it has some magnificent views of the Kedarnath and Kedar dome peaks. It's on the way to Chopta (India's most beautiful ridge), which used to be an old pilgrimage route from Badri to Kedar and is full of medicinal plants. The fields next to the guesthouse belonged to a family who grew potatoes and other seasonal vegetables. They also worked on paddy fields. Ukimath doesn't even get one car a day in terms of traffic, so pollution is close to zero. The people are content and the place has such amazing vibrations that it can lift the spirits of the most depressed and sadelu person on earth. So if you live there and eat jeera alu and roti and some more jeera alu and roti and don't eat supplements, you will not have nutrient deficiencies. Because everything you eat is locally grown and your state of mind is calm, peaceful, content.

My host at a homestay in Sikkim boasted, 'Other than oil and salt, everything on your plate I grow.' He had served me palak soup, radish and squash sabzis, aachar and rice. Himalayan locals eat so much more fibre than we do. Fibre is high in unprocessed foods and thus retains most of its nutrients. In fact all people who live close to nature eat in that way. We don't. And that's why we need supplements. The processed food we eat and the pace of our life is taking all the nutrients away from our food.

To reiterate, there are only two kinds of people who can afford to live without supplements: those who live in a super salubrious place and can trace the origin of their vegetables, fruits, grains (the lucky few who own farms and nurse a passion for growing their own food) and those who have no intention of keeping good health.

Water

Water is the most important nutrient in your body (for survival) without which this chapter is a pure waste of time and paper. Water is the primary transporter of nutrients in the body. Without water you can't use the nutrients that come from carbs, protein and fat. About 70% of the human body is water. We can survive upto 5 weeks without food but less than 5 days without water. (People who were stuck inside the Taj hotel during the recent terrorist attack resorted to drinking water from the AC duct).

Our lifestyle is dehydrating, really. We consume too much of processed food, drink too many teas, coffees and wines. Not to mention the aerated and the non aerated sugary drinks. Even a small drop in the water content of the body lowers our blood volume (enough to get the kidneys and heart over worked). This increases the sodium content in our blood which triggers the thirst response. Sadly, most of us drink only enough to quench our thirst or to wet a dry throat. Not enough to meet our body's water requirement. What's worse? Increase in age, inactivity and stress dulls our thirst mechanism and also lowers the water reserve in our body. All this together leaves us dehydrated most of the time (also a major cause of bloating, by the way).

Water and weight loss

Crash dieting takes the biggest toll on the water reserves in our body. Loss of water is one of the biggest issues that I have against crash dieting and its associated 'guaranteed' weight loss'. Crash dieting which restricts nutrient and water intake (don't let anybody fool you that 3 fruits and 6 juices give you your daily fill) leads to rapid water loss from the body. This on the weighing scale will show itself as weight loss (and on some of the body composition measurement machines as increase in metabolic rate).

This drop in body weight is not reduction of body fat but loss of all important water. Loss of water impairs circulation (now you know why stretch marks are associated with crash dieting), reduces muscle tone, joint and bone health and obviously overworks the kidney, heart and lungs. Oh, yes, it will also lead to body odour because composition of sweat changes.

Losing weight is no big deal, if you lose body water. Body builders and wrestlers routinely adopt this practice. They bring their weight down by as much as 4 kilos on the day prior to a competition. This allows them to compete in a lower weight group and improves their chances of winning. This practice can even lead to death. But body builders and wrestlers have a chance of winning medals. What will you win with rapid weight loss? Stretch marks or chronic fatigue?

A dehydrated condition means that our kidneys have a hard time metabolising our wastes (we can poison ourselves with the wastes that we produce, water is the agent through which we throw these wastes out of the body). Enzymes, digestion, circulation even fat loss are slaves to adequate levels of hydration in our body. Muscles will not contract (commonly felt as cramps or dull aches), joints will hurt and skin will look dull without water (ever seen a stressed out person's skin?). Oh what am I forgetting? Lungs and heart obviously can't breathe or beat without adequate water.

In our bijli, sadak, pani driven democracy—water, without doubt is the clincher. Life without bijli (not Yana Gupta guys) and sadak can be easily coped up with. (In fact some of us city people actually look forward to going to places without bijli and sadak for holiday). But can you live (much less holiday) without water? NO.

FYI—Treks, which are essentially places without sadak and bijli, need to have adequate pani. Places that don't have fresh water streams or good quality water do not become popular trekking routes. All camps en route a trek are by a water source.

Hot water reduces body fat and cold water increases obesity are some of the silliest arguments ever. Water for heavens sake does much more than fat loss.

How much water should you drink? Drink enough so that your urine is always crystal clear, not light yellow, dark yellow or reddish. There are many ways in which water escapes from the body—urine, excretion, sweat, breathing. The only way to hydrate ourselves is by sipping water all the time and by eating wholesome unprocessed food.

So, don't wan't muscle aches, joint problems,

bloating, obesity or dull skin? Reach out for water. And drink beyond quenching your thirst. In fact drink water all the time, sip by sip, swirl it in your mouth like a good wine and let it move down your throat into your stomach. Relish every sip of it. Water is life. Blessed are thou who have good quality water flowing through your taps. The next time you feel sorry for yourself (for whatever reason) remind yourself of the biggest blessing that you are enjoying in this life: 24 hour (or most of the time) good quality water in your taps. It nourishes your being and makes life itself possible.

Honey lime water/apple vinegar cider

The 2 magical drinks which help people melt fat and get them thin. Really? How come most of our aam junta is still FAT? Get off it people, there is really NO magic drink, pill, potion, etc which will burn fat for you.

Honey, if sourced from the right place, has medicinal properties. But if you are taking it without supervision, it can do you more harm than good. Honey, being high in fructose, is not good for those who are insulin insensitive or have high triglyceride or LDL levels. So, do check before you start to have it regularly; it's not right for everyone.

Nimbu can actually work against you. For certain body compositions it can increase headaches, acidity and can create digestion problems. (And it's not the richest source of vitamin C. A guava has much more vitamin C than a lemon or an orange.)

Apple cider: great for cleaning stains and toilets but can cause burning in your throat, irritability and nervousness.

The fact that you are supposed to take these magic potions on an empty stomach, first thing in the morning, exposes you to the hazards all the more.

Otherwise, honey, nimbu and cider when used in diluted forms and as a part of a recipe can enhance flavour and taste. So I am not against these foods per se, just against the mentality that is turning them into what they are not!

4

The 4 principles of
eating right

Standing in front of the mirror every morning, first
thing on rising, Kavita notices a small pimple in her
T zone. Hmm, just PMS, she assures herself. Her
eyes now start wandering and observing beyond
her face. The chin is slightly double. She changes
the angle that she is standing at and now faces the
mirror again. 'My chin looks double from the side
not from the front,' she tells herself. She faces the
mirror again. My boobs sag. My stomach is ok
though. She takes a deep breath in and sucks the
stomach in; it looks dramatically better. Kavita half
smiles and pinches her stomach. She can feel the
flesh in her palms. Not wanting to look down, she
still does and says, 'Yucks, it's easily more than 3
inches of fat.' She now looks at her lower abs: 'This
looks like a ring around my stomach.' And now
the hips: chalo, stand at an angle again. Squeezing
her hips she thinks: 'This is how they should look
even normally.' Lets go of her hips: the fleshy part
falls towards the sides and down. 'Not like this.'
She touches her hips, with her shocking pink nails,
'I wish I had no stretchmarks.' Goes down to the

thighs, the outside are ok, the inside is just so... just so jiggly wiggly. 'Oh no I am so depressed!'

The physical body, what we can see in the mirror is called annamaya kosha according to yoga or yogic philosophy (roughly translated as food body). It's a straight reflection of 'anna' or the food we eat and what time we eat it.

To bring about a difference in the way we look in the mirror, we have to change what and when we eat. Endless scrutiny and criticism of this physical body will always lead us to move away from reality. To look leaner, toned and healthy we just have to follow the 4 most basic principles of eating right.

Principle 1

Never wake up to tea or coffee.

Instead eat real food within 10 to 15 minutes of waking up.

Real life example: 'Look, I can do whatever you want me to do, but I can't give up chai,' pleaded Elvis. 'I just can't. I will die. You know I am in a state of coma every morning, and the only way I get going is through a hot cup of chai. Do you understand?' Elvis, was getting desperate. 'Why don't you wear a white sari and get a halo around your head? Cutting down drinking is fine. But not having chai in the morning is not done ya. I will die. And mine is not the Indian chai which is boiled endlessly with tons of sugar. It's very light, with one, no adha, chamach milk. And I am using a sugar substitute but I can give that up too. And I will cut down to half a cup. Look without tea, I can't even go to the loo. You can't do this... Do you understand? Say something.'

'Ok, give me a chance to talk then,' I said.

'Ok, talk, and say yes to tea baby. Stop being difficult.'

All that I had suggested was no tea first thing in the morning. It scared the shit out of Elvis. Well, it is a scary proposition for most of us. Tea in the morning has a special meaning in each of our lives. Most of us are ready to do 'anything that it takes' to lose weight. But the fact that chai or coffee could be coming in the way of our fat loss doesn't even cross our mind.

I always think of a painting by MF Hussain each time I have the morning cup conversation with a client. It is of a sari-clad lady flying (almost like a super woman), carrying a hot cup of chai against the backdrop of the snowy peaks of the Himalaya. The painting hung in the study of actress Tanvi Azmi (easily amongst the prettiest and bubbliest women in this world) and I couldn't take my eyes off it. It covered almost half her wall and I thought it was beautiful, although I couldn't understand it. Intrigued (it was also the first Hussain painting that I was seeing in flesh and blood; all I knew about him was that his paintings cost the earth, and when you see them you can't make out anything immediately), I asked Tanvi, 'What is this? Why the cup in the woman's hand?'

'Oh, that is my mother-in-law,' said Tanvi smiling.

'I love this painting. But what does it mean?'

Tanvi explained. 'My father-in-law and my mother-in-law both lead very busy lives. They may not see much of each other throughout the day but they have a morning ritual. They always have the morning cup of tea together.' So on one of their anniversaries, Tanvi's father-in-law, the great poet Kaifi Azmi, had written a poem for his wife which went something like this: 'The love that we share over our hot cup of tea every morning, it melts the snows of the mighty Himalaya.' And as he was reading out this poem to his wife, Hussain painted this.

'Wow, how romantic,' I thought. Kaifi Azmi is no more and Hussain is out of the country but the painting remains vivid in my memory.

I know that it takes a lot to give up on that morning chai, but it's worth all the trouble. And the good news is that you don't have to give up on it totally. You can still enjoy the romance, 'me time' or whatever the morning cup means to you. Just make sure that you eat something before that. Why such a fuss? Let me explain.

When you sleep, your blood sugar levels drop in the night. (Babies always wake up in the night, crying, asking to be fed, right? They wake up when their blood sugar drops.) In the morning our liver stores are almost empty. So our blood sugar is low and it's our responsibility to bring this up to an optimum level. Low blood sugar is also a reason why we feel 'low' in the morning. The body sometime takes to wasting or breaking our muscle down to keep our sugar from dropping to abnormally low levels. Not a very good thing if you want to lose weight. To be able to burn fat effectively, you have to train your body to preserve lean tissue (muscle); not waste it by breaking it down into glucose to keep your blood sugar up. What happens in the night is out of our control because we are sleeping, but when we wake up everything is in our control. So, to keep our body's fat burning tissue (muscle) alive—we must eat. Eat real food. Something that will lead to a slow, steady increase in our blood sugar levels. This kicks in the action of insulin, which is secreted by the body as a response to an increase in blood sugar levels, which facilitates our hungry cells to get the nutrients that it is craving for.

Tea or coffee doesn't fit the bill for many reasons. Any stimulant like tea or coffee, which has caffeine (in all varieties; with milk or without, with sugar or without, oolong, white, green, purple, blue) and cigarettes jolt the system out of slumber. It increases the blood pressure, heart rate, breathing rate and makes the body feel stressed or 'kicked'. Sadly we mistake this for feeling awake. In reality, the body experiences stress because of the increase in its heart and breathing rate and will respond by hampering fat burning. **It's important to remember at all times (while fighting with your spouse, getting frustrated by traffic, overworking, etc) that stress is the biggest enemy of an efficient digestive system and of the fat**

burning processes of the body. In the morning, the heart and breathing rates are at its lowest as this is the reflection of a relaxed state of mind and body. To keep the system relaxed, we need to give it real food, which is easy on the heart, lungs and stomach too.

The stimulants provided through tea and coffee increase blood sugar levels but provide zero nutrition to the cells that have been starving for the last 9 to 10 hours or more, post dinner. Moreover, the cuppa can mask your hunger, so you go hungry for a long time without realising it. Going hungry in the morning is a disaster for anybody who dreams of a sexy body. All it does is create a huge calorie deficit in the morning and then the body has no other option but to overeat later to make up for the deficit. All of us who just 'don't feel like eating anything in the morning' are victims of a slow metabolic rate and of a digestive system which is not functioning effectively. Numerous studies have shown how a hearty, healthy breakfast can increase our metabolic rate. Some of the herbal infusions won't give you the caffeine kick but it will prolong the time between waking up and eating, which is why I prefer you stick with this rule even if you are a herbal tea drinker.

Tea and antioxidants

Now isn't your cup of green tea rich in antioxidants? Actually let's understand this whole antioxidants business. Antioxidants are nothing but compounds (mostly vitamins and minerals) which prevent damage from free radicals in the body. (Free radicals are by-products of normal metabolic reactions and are carcinogenic in nature.) Now, the antioxidants can only work in the presence of carbs, proteins and fats. So if that cuppa is going to delay your meal (rich in these macro nutrients), the antioxidants, my dahlings, will be rendered useless!

So like the Vishnu in the Padmanabham temple conveys, look at the picture in totality. Without first eating your meal (which also by the way has vitamins/minerals—source of our beloved antioxidants) your antioxidant rich chai is well, shall I break your heart, useless. By the way, for you to really benefit from the 'antioxidants' you need a large enough amount of them. So it means that you will have to drink many teas, which will only cause acidity, heart burn, bloating, mask your hunger and make you over eat at a later time.

One more heart breaker, when you eat antioxidant rich chocolates (yeah even the dark chocolate variety) the excess sugar or sweetener in it renders the antioxidants in it useless.

With sunrise, the metabolism peaks and the cells demand nutrition. This is the time to eat and to eat big. If you are not used to eating anything in the morning, start with a fruit. After that, within an hour, have your paratha, muesli, dosa, idli, upma, poha, roti and sabzi. Anything that is healthy and fibre rich. Once your cells receive nutrition through food and the blood sugar comes to an optimum level, feel free to have your tea or coffee. The breathing rate, heart rate, etc will still increase, but now your first meal or breakfast will act as a buffer.

So the foundation to a great body is laid by what you eat and drink (or not) within the first 10 to 15 minutes of waking up. Eating right is about getting in touch with your body and sharpening your awareness of it. Eating immediately on rising puts us in touch with our body's hunger signals. Instead of going through an afternoon slump we will start feeling hungry more often in the day. Which leads us to the second principle.

But before that what about going to the loo? When you follow all the four principles, you will actually want to go to the loo first thing in the morning even before you eat or drink anything. 'Prabhate mal darshanam': witness, or see, your shit every morning. I will explain how and why this happens at the end of this chapter. In the rare case that you can't go, you will feel like doing so after eating your first meal because it will increase the peristalsis, or the movement of your intestines, signalling you to go.

The Asian pot

Hey, I am talking about the one you have in the toilet. After we have sat on our pot, read our paper, bent forward to put 'pressure' on our eliminatory organs (actually a way to imitate or recreate a more natural position), we get up (not so satisfied, feeling like 'something is still in there') and wash our hands using a 'natural' hand wash which has not been tested on animals and uses natural herbs. On one hand, we want everything ayurvedic, herbal, natural (green tea, herbal infusions, spas, even ayurvedic clothes) and on the other hand we use the most unnatural posture for defecation. But if we care so much for natural, how about adopting the most natural (and comfortable) squatting posture when we answer 'nature's call'?

The seated posture on the western toilet actually closes and constricts your eliminatory organs. Under pressure or stress, it's almost impossible to feel 'open to let go'. This then leads to the vicious cycle of laxatives, which further weakens your digestive system and washes off all the B vitamins from the large intestine. So all that you do is 'create' problems for yourself. Western toilets and the discomfort they bring to the body have been identified as a contributor to constipation, colon cancers, and irritable bowel syndrome.

The traditional Indian shitting posture (actually this is exactly what everybody used before the advent of the commode, including Westerners), helps you relax the organs and encourages you to let go. This posture will also help you get rid of bloating. A clear stomach and a digestive system which works at its optimal health are the foundation of losing fat and getting healthier.

Of course, to get comfortable in the Indian sitting posture you will need to workout regularly to keep those hips and legs strong and flexible and the joints lubricated. (It's sad how inactivity has made this most natural posture impossible for us.)

Come on, its not enough to assert that we are all Indians only after a terror attack or during an India-Pak match, we need to do it daily, in our own private space, the bathroom. So say yes to sitting the Indian way. Oh, I can almost see you nodding the Indian way!

As for aesthetics, if your designer is good, the bathroom will look great either way!

Summary

Eating first thing in the morning will lead to an

- Increase in blood sugar and energy levels, which will lead to an...
- Increase in metabolic rate and fat burning, and a...
- Decrease in acidity and bloating, and will...
- Reduce chances of overeating later in the day, and...
- Stabilise blood sugar levels throughout the day, which means...
  Less chances of getting fat.

Principle 2

Eat every 2 hours.

First things first. You will be able to follow principle 2 only if you follow principle 1. Without step 1 you will not be in a position to reach step 2. Eating first thing in the morning lays the foundation for us to efficiently receive hunger signals from our body. It teaches us to be fearless about eating. Too many of us fear eating. 'If I eat, I will become fat,' we think. Now, how have we come to this conclusion? Most of us can identify with this pattern: 'I don't really feel hungry in the morning, even lunch I barely have, but after 5 pm I don't know what happens. That's the time I call for biscuits, pizza, sev puri, golgappa, vada pav, samosa, burger, etc. Basically anything that I can lay my hands on. So till that time I am eating healthy and watching my diet, after that I don't know. It's almost like split personality. One way of eating (not eating) from 10 am to 5 pm and a diametrically opposite way of eating (overeating) from 5 pm to 10 pm.'

Even if you remotely belong to this category, the thought of eating every 2 hrs will make you feel restless. 'Boss, I can never eat so much.'

But what you are completely overlooking is that you eat a lot at one time. Now the question is, can we show the smartness to eat multiple times in a day instead of 2 to 3 times?

'Hey, I barely have time for breakfast, and I skip lunch most of the time or have it by 3.30 or 4 pm, so I don't have the time to eat so many times in the day.' The problem here is that our stomach doesn't understand that we have meetings, conferences, deadlines, presentations, fixed lunch hours, etc. And it is on a mission to remain true to its dharma. So it keeps secreting hydrochloric acid and keeps asking you to eat. But we are smarter than the stomach; the minute it sends us the signal to eat we either give it a tea, coffee, cigarette, mint, pan masala or chewing gum, etc (depending on our taste) and almost always choose not to eat, trying to stave off those hunger pangs as long as possible. The stomach may feel like a neglected child, but we have better things to do than feeding it. When the hunger signal becomes unbearable we finally suffocate the stomach with so much food that we progressively work at weakening it; and therefore the hunger signals that it can send to our brain. Eating frequent meals every 2 hours is not just better for our digestive system, but it keeps us from overeating.

Amrita Arora never believed in dieting. Then she saw her best friend Kareena eat every 2 hours and looking better and leaner than ever before. 'Bebo's like clockwork, man. She takes this super quick 5 minute break even while she is in the shot, eats and gets back to delivering a stunning performance. While we were shooting together, she would go like "Accha chalo, 5 mins to 4 pm, it's my peanut time." I am just so impressed with her discipline, ya. She is eating all the time and looking like a million bucks.'

Amu had to shoot for a magazine cover and she needed a flat stomach for it. 'Listen, I don't know if I can be like Bebo, she is too good ya, I don't know if I can eat every do-do ghanta'.

'Look, if you want to have a flat stomach, you will have to eat every 2 to max 2 ½ hours. For a flat stomach like Bebo's, you need her discipline much more than her dietician.'

'Point noted,' said Amu.

So what else does eating often do for you? First of all, every time you eat your body has to work at breaking the food down, digesting it and absorbing it. This process is called DIT or Diet Induced Thermogenesis. In simple English, it means more calorie burning. Now you thought only gymming, running, cycling burns calories. Surprise, surprise, eating helps you burn calories too. The more often you eat, the more you can utilise DIT. Which means that every 2 hours, you can increase your calorie burning just by eating.

The idea of eating every 2 hours may sound ridiculous, but only if you are imagining the size of your meals right now and thinking 'My god, if I eat like this 6 to 7 times in the day, I will look like an elephant.' But when you adopt the idea of eating frequently, often what drops first is the size of the meal. You will then find it impossible to eat that pizza by yourself. One piece and you will feel full; 2 chapatis for lunch at 2 pm when you just had something at noon is difficult too. So you may land up eating just 1 chapati at 2 pm and the next one at 4 pm.

When you eat every 2 hours a day, it's a given that you will eat small. So the number of calories you consume at one time will be very small. When our body gets a regular dose of a small number of calories often, through the day, it feels reassured and loved. Eating is a way of loving our body and providing it with nourishment. Not eating for long hours (more than 3) or starving is an act of punishment, like being angry at ourselves. When our body gets fewer calories at a time, they are utilised better and not stored as fat. Also, because the body is feeling reassured with a regular intake of calories and nutrients, it sees no reason to store body fat. The body loses fear of death due to starvation (which is instilled by a combination of prolonged gaps between meals and eating a lot at one time), and feels encouraged to let go of its fat stores (which it has been holding on to as its means of survival).

So in short, eating after every 2 hours will lead to

- A conducive environment in the body to burn fat
- Fewer calories converted to fat
- Less dependence on stimulants
- Smarter thinking, because the brain gets a regular flow of sugar
- Flatter stomach, no need to hold on to fat stores

And what happened to Amu? She shot for the magazine cover looking super hot. And she was pleasantly shocked that her stomach looked so flat.

'I am very happy with you, Rujuta,' said Amu's mother, who was earlier sceptical about the whole 'diet business' (typical mom). 'She is eating at regular intervals and most importantly her coffee has reduced from 6 cups a day to barely 2. That is the best thing about this diet.'

'Now Mom, you go on a diet with Rujuta,' said Amu. (Typical daughter.)

Now, how does this work? It's actually not as complicated as it sounds. All we're doing is taking our 3 main meals (breakfast, lunch and dinner), cutting the portions, and then adding some in between meals to these core meals. Let's say that you start with fruit for meal 1. And you can have any traditional healthy meal for breakfast: upma, idli, dosa, puri bhaaji, aloo paratha. After that eat no more than 3 things for lunch: for example, roti + sabzi + dal OR rice + curd + sabzi, or any other combination you like (avoid meat if you're working as this will slow you down) and reduce one thing from dinner. So keep dinner as just roti + sabzi OR dal + sabzi (here you can have your meat, your non-veg).

For all the in between meals, eat only one thing at a time: peanuts, cheese, nuts, milk, yogurt, soy milk or whey protein shakes. These foods are wholesome and are higher in protein content, which we are always in danger of being deficient in. They stabilise blood sugar, help you think faster and support sedentary activities without getting converted to fat, importantly. When I consult, I recommend particular things to particular clients, but what I have outlined works as a general guideline.

Ok, how do you find time to eat? Well, when you eat 6 to 7 times in the day, it really doesn't take too much time. Just a couple of minutes. The kind of small meal I am asking you to eat is a handful of peanuts, a bowl of yoghurt, a slice or wedge of cheese. These are all foods you can keep in the office fridge, or in your desk. The 5:30 to 7 pm main meal is something you need to plan for, however, just as you plan your lunch. In the last chapter, I give you a variety of options which will make it easier for you but eating every 2 hours means you do need to plan ahead.

And this is my theory: we work to feed our stomachs. We educate ourselves, put all our effort into making good money so that we and our loved ones can lead a secure and fulfilling life. The irony is that our stomach is left feeling insecure. It's clueless about where, when and how its next meal will come. We may get driven in or drive big cars, have huge houses, designer clothes, LV bags and Jimmy Choo shoes, but we don't pay the same attention to our stomach, which is collecting fat for survival and always stressed about its next meal. So make time and connect with your stomach. Food is the way to do it.

Real life example:
Only busy people make time for everything.

Samir Bhatia of Barclays Bank leads a very busy life. He's been running for a long time and it's his passion, and he came to me because he wanted to run better and faster. Samir has deadlines, presentations, travels overseas, etc more than anybody else I know. Once, he travelled from the east coast to the west coast of America, and then went on to London, Hongkong and Mauritius, all in 20 days! He still stuck to the diet just as planned. I am blessed with sincere and devoted clients like him.

He told me the strategy he uses to stick to eating every 2 hours. The meals, of course, were planned in consideration of his place, schedule, everything; but how much he would land up following, especially through presentations and seminars, I really doubted. But Samir is brilliant. He would carry his meals in the pocket of his designer suit. 'When it was my time to eat, I would excuse myself, saying that I had to go to the loo. And on my way to the restroom, I would eat my channa, cheese, etc.'

Wow, I was so touched. I can almost see Samir walking through a 5 star lobby towards the restroom, munching his food.

All my clients report that they start working much better and faster once they eat often. I am not surprised, are you?

Principle 3

Eat more when you are more active and less when you are less active

Always fine-tune your eating to your activity. But remember, principle 3 cannot be followed without principle 2. Only when you eat all the time can you actually decrease meal size when less active and increase it when more active.

Once you follow principles 1 and 2, principle 3 will just naturally follow. Principles 1 and 2 put you in touch with your hunger signals and train you to listen and follow them. Just like when you drive your car more, you need more petrol, but when it's parked it just needs enough to start (without any trouble) and to last till your next destination or the closest petrol pump. When you are in touch with your system, it will want more food when it is more active, and less food when it is not so active.

With the sunrise in the morning, the body's metabolic rate picks up. Which means that sitting and reading in the morning is a bigger calorie burner than sitting and reading in the evenings. The metabolic rate is higher in the morning than it is post sunset. So even the act of sitting will burn more calories. It goes without saying that you should eat more in the morning. And your stomach will feel free to communicate that with you once you encourage an open dialogue with it, through principles 1 and 2.

We get fat only because we don't give a damn about what the stomach needs, and load or unload it according to our convenience. If deprivation of food is punishment then overeating is a crime. You will see in the next chapter of diet recall (Chapter 5, 'Inculcating awareness'), how most of us get fat only because we eat at the wrong time and do not eat at the right time. If we don't eat food when the body needs it, all this does is create a huge calorie and nutrient deficit. Later, when the time is wrong, that is the metabolic processes are slowing down, your body and mind will demand a lot of food to make up for the deficit.

Time is very important. Time once lost will never come back. The popular serial *Mahabharat* had samay or time as its sutradhar. 'Time, time ki baat hai jhonny,' sang Helen very philosophically. Lives can be saved by a few seconds, relationships can be mended if things are done on time, wounds are healed with time. Time is indeed precious and divine. Goddess Kali, one of the most important goddesses of India, is the representation of time. And body rhythms are supposed to be the work of Kali. Thus a way to respect time, is to respect body rhythms.

Time of the day and activity affect our calorie burning. Each one of us has a pattern to our day that we must make a wholehearted attempt to understand, if we wish to stay lean and fit for life. Mornings lead to higher calorie burning in the body because nature designed us that way. It's nature's way of getting us ready. Time even affects what we do outside the body, outside of our immediate selves. Now, 9 am in the morning could be workout time for some, conference time, reporting time, school time, etc for others; 5.30 pm could be tuition time, meeting time, break or head back home time for some. But with the BPO boom in India some of us are actually leaving for work at 10.30 pm and heading back home at 7 am. Alternately, homemakers find time for themselves after husband, father-in-law and children are packed off to work and school respectively. Once we understand the pattern of our day, we can plan what to eat and how much.

A lot of foods have a tarnished reputation only because they have been routinely eaten at the wrong times. Laddoos, especially the homemade ones (though Gita Bhavan of Rishikesh gives tough competition to the homemade variety), with fibre rich grain, ghee, dry fruits and the most important ingredient, ma ka pyar, if eaten as a meal in the morning can put any cereal and milk, toast and beans, omelette, etc to shame. But we either carry them to office and share it with the gang post lunch or save them in the fridge and eat them as dessert post dinner. At both these times they are eaten post meal instead of as a meal in itself. And because laddoos are dense in calories, if they are eaten with a meal or late at night, no prizes for guessing: they are converted to fats, and all the nutrients are wasted. The body cannot absorb nutrients on an overloaded stomach (post meal) or when it is slowing down (post sunset).

Cheese, pasta, paratha, peanuts, paneer, banana, mango, potato, rice, etc are misunderstood only because you have experienced them at the wrong time in your day. None of these foods are fattening. They are just dense in energy (calories) or fat (which as you read, you will understand is healthy and crucial for life itself). In fact, I will go to the extent of saying that **no food is fattening. You have to just be smart enough to choose the right time to eat it.**

High activity could mean both physical and mental activity; for example, going to the gym or any kind of physical exercise, cooking, doing intensive thinking, attending important meetings, organising weddings, shifting houses. In short, any activity where you are very actively involved and that demands a lot of energy from you. Times of stress, travelling, and illness would also be high demand periods. And not just for you. If you're ill, then your family or near ones will go through a time where they expend energy.

Low activity means any time you are passive, or relatively inactive, not using your mental energies; watching a movie or TV, surfing the net, making small talk on the phone, checking emails, doing low intensive admin work (such as paying bills and signing checks), being driven around, going out to a party (unless you are dancing quite a bit), napping, delegating work; in short any routine work.

We need to up our eating during high demand periods and cut down when relaxing.

Not just this, the cells of our body become less sensitive to nutrition and calories if they have not been active. So when you are just chilling, the cells become dull, they don't want anything (they're in no mood to absorb nutrients and see no reason to make energy demands); so if you load your stomach at this time, it just gets converted to fat. But post activity (mental or physical) the cells are energy and nutrient deprived. This increases their sensitivity, which means that whatever you eat will get used up to replenish those hungry cells and not get converted to fat.

If you lack enthusiasm or energy it's just because you are eating more when you are less active and vice versa. Can you identify with any one of these situations: a) You really want to watch this movie. Your friend books the tickets on the internet. You have had a normal day at work or home, nothing exceptional, but instead of feeling enthusiastic about going to the theatre you think, ok, can I go on Saturday afternoon, or maybe catch it later when it's released on TV? b) You have to go for dinner at a cousin's place. You are really looking forward to spending some time with your cousin, but on the evening of the dinner you think, 'It's too far off. Maybe I can do it on another day?'

It's not that you are lazy (only your mom, dad, and spouse think so), sick or psycho (only you think that you are) it's just that sometimes you are not 'up to' things. You really want to get out of home but when it actually comes to the crunch, your enthu or motivation is low.

Look at your eating and activity pattern. If there is a disconnect or disproportion between your meal size and level of activity, you will be affected by the 'not being up to it' syndrome. It's also called a sub clinical deficiency (well documented condition again), which means that you are not sick but lack optimal health. A simple way to get rid of this 'don't know what's happening to me ya' feeling is to eat more when your cells are more sensitive (which is when activity is higher, in the earlier part of the day) and eat less when less active. In the ideal world we should have finished having our 2 main meals by 11 am, especially if we have a weight issue.

Real life example:

Suman, a homemaker, started working with her husband when his business hit on bad times. She had moved 3 cities and delivered 2 babies by the time she shifted to Mumbai. She didn't know how, but in 8 years she went up from 80 kilos to 125 kilos. She was careful about what she ate and ate very little. Woke up at 6 am and had a chai. Worked out at 8 am after packing off kids, and had another chai. Then at 10 am, she would have poha, upma or khakra. Then, depending on when she would get free at work, between 2 to 4 pm, she would have her lunch, which was 1 or 2 rotis, sabzi, dal. And then sukha bhel sometimes, or 2 biscuits by 6 to 7 pm, and then dinner just like lunch: 2 rotis, sabzi, dal and of course a little rice if very hungry.

If you look at her food, she is not doing anyting so drastically wrong that she should have become 125 kilos, but the timings are all off. Suman doesn't see herself as important, and prioritises everything before herself. Look at what she's doing: she doesn't put a thing in her stomach until 10 am, but she's been up since 6 am and in fact very active: she's cooked and worked out. Her lunch timings are uneven, and she is having it pretty late. Her snacks are utterly non-nutritious and most importantly, she is doing most of her eating from late afternoon, when her body isn't in a position to utilise this food. Moreover, because she hasn't fed her body in the morning, her metabolism has slowed down. In fact, because she hasn't eaten during the high activity times of her day, her body has gone on conservation mode; ie, thinking that it's starving, the body lowers the metabolic rate and starts to conserve all the fat.

To summarise

- Eating more food when you're more active will make your body an efficient calorie burner...
- Which will increase the metabolic rate of your body...
- Which will help you stay energetic through the day...
- And will help you lose fat more effectively.

Principle 4

Finish your last meal at least 2 hours prior to sleeping.

Simply an extension of principle 3. We need to start eating less post sunset and as our activities wind down.

What are you doing just before sleeping? Generally unwinding and watching TV, reading, chatting, etc. Basically your activity is lower than what it was in the morning, so is your metabolism, and the digestion capacity of your stomach.

One of the most dangerous habits that we have developed is not eating dinner unless it's really late. People come back home after work and for some strange reason don't feel like eating dinner. Everybody wants to have nashta (preferably fried: farsan and chips, biscuits, or anything else which is salty) and then have dinner while watching their favourite serial. (Prime time is 9 to 9.30 pm.) This

168

obviously loads your stomach. The best thing to do is to eat a healthier or fuller meal by 6 to 6.30 pm in the evening, and then eat really light by 8 to 8.30 pm.

Remember, digesting food is a calorie burner and work for the body. In the night, cells are naturally not very sensitive to energy or nutrients as they don't really need much so if you overload your stomach most of it will get wasted or converted to fat. You may eat the healthiest of food but the body has to be in a mood to digest and absorb nutrients from it.

The worst thing is of course eating a lot and then sleeping immediately. Just like khali pet pe neend nahi aati, overloaded stomach pe disturbed sleep aati hai.

A good quality, restful and peaceful sleep is the backbone to losing fat. While we sleep, our body repairs cells (the same reason why you invest in expensive night creams), balances the hormones, rejuvenates the cells of our body, repairs the damage that we have put our cells through during the day, and gets ready for the next day. Without peaceful sleep, your hormones or your lean tissue will not be able to support fat burning. Stress or disturbed sleep throw the hormones off balance, and depletes us of lean tissue (muscle breakdown and bones thinning), both of which hamper fat burning.

In the night, when we sleep, our system or the body's intelligence should feel free to do what it is supposed to do: repair wear and tear and rejuvenate. If at this time the stomach is overloaded, the body is torn between two things. Our body's recovery system takes a beating and the food doesn't get broken down, digested and absorbed properly. End result: you wake up feeling not just tired and weary (recovery process hampered), but also with a bloated stomach, swollen face, acidity, burping (digestion hampered); generally feeling heavy and dull, instead of fresh and light.

My diet plans usually get me two immediate reactions: 1) How can I eat so much in the day? 2) How can I eat so little in the night?

Which is followed by the inevitable question, 'What if I feel hungry after the last meal? Give me options to eat.'

To which my standard response is: 'Call me if you feel hungry.'

'Even if its midnight or 3 am?'

'Ya, whatever time, my phone is on all the time.'

I am yet to get any call from a client. I usually get smses which typically read something like: 'Can I skip dinner?'; 'Too full'; 'Losing interest in the last meal'; 'Never dreamt that I would want to not have heavy dinner'.

Workout late evenings

Some people I know workout late evening, but because they want to eat light for dinner, eat nothing post workout. Well this is the deal: a pre workout and post workout meal is a necessity irrespective of the time of the day you workout at. So even if its a 8 pm or 10 pm workout, make sure you have your high GI carbs and protein shake within 10 minutes of working out. Yup, even if it's 11 pm.

If you look at your current lifestyle, reducing the size of dinner and having it early may (and rightly so) sound like an impossible proposition. Eating the last meal 2 hours before bedtime is crucial for long term health, change in body composition (increase in muscle and bone weight, decrease in fat weight), that glowing complexion (Acne free. Ever visited a skin doctor? The first thing they want to know is if your stomach is clear.) and a restful sleep. But it requires serious and permanent change in lifestyle. Without principles 1, 2 and 3, principle 4 cannot be employed, and in fact will fall flat.

When you sleep just right (the ideal time to sleep is between 10 and 10:30 pm to 5 am and you should stick as close to this as you can), it will show on your body, face and health. Some people suffer from stretchmarks (women on their thighs, hips, stomach, and men on the chest and arms) post weight loss. When weight loss comes without healthy changes in lifestyle, stretchmarks are just one of the signs of abuse that you have put your body through. If you want no stretchmarks or want to reduce the ones you already have, eat 2 hours before bedtime.

TV out of the bedroom

Gul and Naveen led hectic schedules and had made a policy decision of not having cable TV at home, to safeguard the kids from all that nonsense. But after they put the kids off to sleep, around 10 pm they watched DVDs (of series like *Seinfeld*, *Lost*, *Friends*, or movies) for a good hour or 2. Naveen never really slept too well; he always had a disturbed sleep. Gul struggled to get out of bed every morning, and was always tired in the morning. Is it rocket science? Not really.

Watching TV is not relaxing, but rather a taxing activity for the body, especially the eyes and the brain. Let's refresh what we learnt in school. We should always look at things on which the light is getting reflected; reading by the window and not staring at the source of light. Now your TV (and laptop) are emitting harsh rays. So your eyes and brain are still stressed, sweetie. And you know what stress does to fat burning. So switch off that TV (including what you watch on DVD) and laptop at least an hour before bedtime. Yes, a book is alright. Just get the lighting right.

When you eat too late (immediately before bedtime) or do the TV and bed dinner, the food remains undigested in your intestines. The area of the small intestine is pretty large, almost the size of 3 tennis courts (next to each other), so there is plenty of scope for your body to absorb nutrients as they make their long journey through it. But if you have eaten more than what is in your capacity to digest (according to yogic philosophy one of the signs of an ignorant man), the undigested food remains in the tract and bacteria act upon it. This can turn the healthiest of meals into toxins.

These toxins (aam, in ayurveda) lead to acidity, bloating, constipation (short term), gain in body fat levels and appearance of stretch marks (long term). The chances of nightmares or scary dreams are high after a big, late dinner, and actually increase after consumption of dessert at night. Dreams are a way for our mind to digest and make sense of all the impressions and information that it has collected in the day. A full stomach interferes with this process too. In short, if you eat like a dog in the night you will behave like a bitch in the day (don't take offence with the gender please).

Now, this principle of eating early will make it easy for us to employ principle 1; which is to eat immediately on rising. If the stomach is heavy, bloated and constipated in the morning, the last thing on your mind is food. A dull, lethargic and tired mind will need a caffeine kick to start the day off. So phut goes your diet plan and with it the permanent fat loss, with that glowing skin, lustrous hair and flat stomach (stretch mark free) that you so yearn for. But once you follow principle 4, you will wake up without the need of an alarm, and your stomach will give you the signal to download. When you enter the bathroom you will be able to defecate without straining and you will walk out of your bathroom feeling light, hungry and happy (not heavy, gassy and irritated).

What about sex?

What about sex, asked my editor. Doesn't that help you digest your meal after dinner? Surely you can eat late and then work it off. Hmmm. Big no. It's the same with taking a walk straight after dinner. When we finish our food, our stomach immediately starts to digest it and needs all its resources to break it down, absorb and assimilate the nutrients. At this time, it needs all the blood supply (in fact, vajrasana, which is a recommended posture post dinner, aids digestion because it directs all the blood flow to the stomach) while during sex, the blood supply goes to your genitals; during your walk, it moves towards your legs and arms. So you think you're working off your food when actually you're obstructing its digestion. My advice to my editor was maximise calorie burning and have sex before dinner!

Why will you feel like going to the loo, first thing in morning? It's because eating light and 2 hours prior to bedtime allows the body plenty of time to digest, absorb and metabolise food correctly. The process of shitting will be so quick that you will not need a book or newspaper to distract or relax. (The parasympathetic nervous system which is responsible for relaxing the entire body allows the sphincters to open and allows for the faeces to move towards the anus.) A light stomach ensures restful and peaceful sleep, so the state of mind is relaxed too.

Prabhate mal darshanam, which I've referred to earlier in this chapter, is a sign of good health and an efficient digestive system. Only a relaxed mind and light (healthy) body has the privilege of the darshan of mal every morning.

At this point I would like to add a little note. Most people like to read (some people have dedicated places for books, magazines and newspapers in the bathroom) while shitting. Don't! Just like for good digestion you don't read, play games on mobile, answer calls, or watch TV while eating, refrain doing all that while shitting too. Stay connected with how and what your body throws out; this is the clue to what to eat and what to avoid. Don't miss out on this crucial lesson.

Get out of the vicious cycle of caffeine and nicotine kicks in the morning, straining on the toilet seat, skipping lunch, not feeling hungry till evening, overeating in the night, getting disturbed sleep at night, and waking up dull and tired in the morning.

The day you wake up feeling hungry and with an urge to clear the stomach, know that you have started on the path of permanent 'results'. Hunger is a sign of youth, health, happiness and peace.

To summarise

To eat 2 hours before bedtime will lead to

- Most of your food being digested before you go to bed...
- Which will lead to sound sleep...
- Which will leave your body free to do its repair work...
- Which will make your body more effective in burning fat.

Bad breath

This is clearly a bigger dampener than a pot belly. Why does it feature in a diet book? Because it's got to do with your food intake and the health of your digestive system. When food is not getting digested properly, it can leave a bad smell in your mouth (falling sick does that too). Lack of digestive enzymes and overeating are big culprits when it comes to making your mouth stink.

Cut the size of your meal down. Follow the principles of increasing nutrient intake, and exercise regularly to keep the digestive system healthy. Increase the amount of water, because dehydration can be smelled from a conversation distance (words smell of 'I need water'). Most of us experience this every morning or after a long flight (not drinking water in the night and pressure controlled conditions of flight increase our chances of dehydration).

A vitamin C supplement will also help. And last but not the least, visit your dentist regularly (once in 6 months) to check for cavities or other issues in your mouth which can alter the way you chew and therefore the way you digest food and experience enzymatic actions. And yeah, do the Indian thing: gargle after every meal. Water will not just hydrate your mouth, but will also act as an cleansing agent in your mouth.

The (Vicious) Cycle of Life

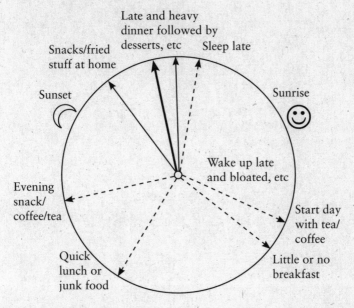

The Four Principles

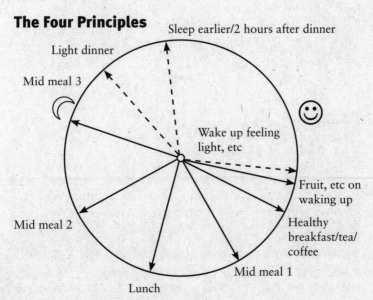

5

Inculcating awareness

As you wait for your turn to pay at your local food mall you might have noticed a huge guy with tons of aerated drinks, jams, butter, biscuits, chips, etc loaded in his cart. While he waits for his turn, he also picks up chewing gums and chocolates which are laid out to tempt buyers exactly in his situation. And you wonder, doesn't he understand that this is wrong? That he can't be eating so much junk?

I come from a typical Konkanastha Brahmin family, where 90% of the people are engineers and the remaining 10% doctors, CAs, bankers and teachers. Earlier at my family functions, what I do for a living used to be a major topic of discussion. Now, the kind of people who seek my advice are a topic of discussion. There is an almost unanimous agreement that people who consult me must be seriously lacking IQ. My family just can't understand how people can get so fat in the first place. And then instead of just cutting down on what they are eating why do they need to seek out 'professional advice'. (We are blessed with a high metabolic rate. My grandfather and his 6 brothers were forced to migrate to Bombay because they were starving in the Konkan. Extreme poverty ensured that genetically we would carry less fat cells. NOW you know why those doctors ask for genetic or family history!)

'You make a living by telling people what to eat?' one of my mamas joked. 'The people who come to you must be crazy. Why should they come and pay you? So that you can tell them to stop eating fried food and sweets. Don't they already know that?' (Now this is typical Kobra—Konkanastha Brahmin —behaviour. It's a community afflicted with a know it all attitude like no other.) So obviously my entire family 'knows' that other than telling them not to eat fried food and sweets, there is nothing more that I do with my clients. At the most I must be telling them to stop eating rice. For this I get paid? Ridiculous.

Information without awareness is useless

Yes it's a fact: everybody knows that they should be avoiding sweets and fried stuff. Everybody. Even your gulli ka kutta. Then how come so many people are still eating them? It's simple: they lack complete awareness about what they are stuffing their mouths with. Information without awareness is like riding a bike with the helmet on the handle. You have the right equipment but it's not in the right place. Useless. Just like the information that eating pizza, chips, chocolates, pastries will make you fat is not enough. What you need is awareness. To develop awareness, you need to start observing what you are doing.

Awareness comes when the mind is in a meditative state. Hmm... now how many times in the day do we catch ourselves in this meditative state? Almost never. A state of meditation is reached (ok for most of us reaching the meditative state in this life is almost impossible), or we can get closer to a meditative state, when we experience a certain amount of calmness in our mind. Many of us lead a life where we had to finish almost everything yesterday, where we are at every moment torn in between 2 or more things or people, where we just don't have the time to do or pursue anything that we even remotely love, and where stress is an inevitable part of our existence.

How then can we go about cultivating awareness? Or is there no hope for us? No, there is hope. And it is called 'Diet recall' in the field of nutrition. A standardised (used world over) 24 hour diet recall requires you to write down everything that you eat and drink from the time you wake up till the time you sleep, along with time, quantity and a brief description of food. A 24 hour diet recall gives you and the nutritionist you are working with a good idea of what you eat at what time, your food likes and dislikes, your calorie and nutrient intake, etc.

I have further modified the standard 24 hour diet recall to suit my clients' needs and lifestyle. I get them to write a **3 day diet and activity recall**. Two of these days are working days and 1 a chutti day, depending on which day of the week is 'off' or 'day out' for you. Typically, most of my clients note down Saturday or Sunday, Monday and Tuesday.

Along with the diet recall I also get them to jot down their activity recall. Which means that they also put down everything that they have done in the day along with what time they did it. So, everything from brushing teeth, driving, meetings; all the gory details. But it doesn't stop here. After diet and activity, they have to put down workout details (if any): weight training, yoga, cardio or whatever.

Why do we need such a lamba-chauda process? To bring ourselves an inch closer towards awareness. If your home loan company promises you a deal or exchange, will a verbal assurance do or do you want that in writing? Writing has that effect on us. You have to think using your mind, your hands write and your eyes see what is written. It creates a much deeper understanding of what we are doing and why we are doing it. (Remember your mother always asked you to write answers in a notebook and not just read them from the text.) When my clients (after initial resistance) agree to write their 3 day diet and activity recall, they are aghast at what they read at the end of three days. About 90% of them swear that these 3 days were unusual, and that on all other days they eat very differently. They don't have as much coffee, eat dinners earlier, don't eat sweets, and workout regularly, blah blah blah...

In my initial years as a nutritionist, I had a hard time getting my clients to write the recall. I have actually lost clients because I have insisted on seeing the diet and activity recall which they were so averse to writing. But today clients are coming to me because I am willing to listen to everything that they do and eat in the day; because I don't pack them off with standardised printouts of diets and pocket an amount for it.

That's not the point though. The point is that food is one of the 4 primitive fountains of life, together with sex, sleep and the instinct for self preservation. Food is instinctive. Food is a means through which we can start on this beautiful journey towards our real spiritual self. 'Anna he purnabramha': this means that food is bramha, a vedantic concept that means completeness or oneness. Food is something through which we can become one with God or with our inner self. And no, this is not a Vedantic or Hindu concept alone. Whatever religion you believe in or were born into, no matter how old or new age the religion is, it will place special emphasis on food.

One of my writer friends has an interesting take on the diet and activity recall: 'Your method is going to force people to move inwards. Only the fearless will opt for your diet plan.' Most people are threatened at the very thought of moving inwards; 99% of my clients offer to verbally tell me what their diet is, or just quickly put down a typical day for me on paper, at the most. This is followed by reassurances, mother promises, etc that their day is exactly like this. (My funniest moment was when a director of a pharma company pulled her throat and said, 'Dekh jooth nahi bolti, itna kheecha hai.'; referring to the skin that she had pulled from the throat.) They have never eaten out of this pattern, they can't, as they are bogged down by working hours, pressures, etc; why I want to waste time with one; why don't I just tell them what to do; they have spent so long being fat, and now they are raring to go and shed the weight; they will do everything as I say; why don't I just tell them what to do. (Most of these people have been through multiple diets where they were just told what to do. They followed them religiously, lost weight, and obviously gained double of it in no time. But have they learnt anything?)

When I insist that to ensure we all save time they come back with their diet recall, they give in reluctantly. Now what I do to keep my client's heart is save the 'typical day' diet recall paper anyway. When they come back with the actual diet recall and we compare them with the typical day, they are as similar as chalk and cheese.

The typical day or what they want to tell me verbally is usually how they would like to see themselves eating, not how they are actually eating. But it is also what they seriously think they are eating. Brings us back to awareness. They are simply unaware that they are eating way different from what they would actually want themselves to be eating. That's exactly why some people believe that they are doing nothing wrong, eat very little, and yet seem to gain weight. It just means that they are unaware of what's wrong. Now, when they have proof in black and white that what they actually ate (reality) is different from their perception, they are shocked, to say the least.

This process, though tedious and difficult (seemingly), is a powerful tool. You will instantly know why you are gaining weight. Just one look at the 3 day diet and activity recall will help you know yourself better. It's a complete, no holds barred revelation. And an amazing one at that.

Although you may not have the skills to read a diet recall like an experienced dietician and use it in the same way, it will be a fun exercise to do. And it's the best way to see if you're lying to yourself. Awareness is the first step towards health and weight loss. (I've given you diet and activity recall forms to fill out for yourself also, in Appendix 3.)

Here are some sample diet and activity recall forms of some of my clients. I have tried to choose diet recalls so as to have a good representation of different professions. I then go on to dissect these recalls to identify patterns which are harmful and are obviously coming in the way of fat loss. Based on the diet recalls, I recommend some changes in their eating pattern, which will help them towards their goal. It might amuse you to see how other people really eat!

Sample diet and activity recalls for specific profiles

Note: All the below diets are only indicative and not actual diets. These are changes that we can bring about in our life without the 'interference' of a nutritionist. Breaking down our diet based on the 4 common sense principles is not an alternative to going to an expert in nutrition science, but it provides for a strong foundation from where professional help can take off.

Profile 1: Rohini, freelance journalist, early 40s

Day 1			
Food/ Drink	Quantity	Activity Recall	Workout
		9.30 am: wake up	6-7 pm Cardio: treadmill 30 minutes
Breakfast: 10 am	Lemon tea with Splenda: 4 cups	10-11.45 am: read papers, check email, etc.	Cross-trainer: 15 minutes
	Sliced papaya: 1 bowl	12 noon: shower and leave house	Fixed weights: 15 minutes

	5 almonds soaked overnight	1.30 pm: lunch at neighbour-hood café	
Lunch: 1.30 pm	Grilled chicken salad with roasted almonds	2.20-3.30 pm: meeting at work	
	Cappucino	4-5.30 pm: Italian class	
	Diet Coke	Coffee at the café at the centre	
Tea: 5.30 pm	Black coffee with 2 biscotti	6-7 pm: workout at the gym	
		7.30-8 pm: On my home computer working	
		8.30-9 pm: fix dinner	
Dinner: 9 pm	Cold meat platter, roasted peppers, lentils	9-10 pm: have dinner, watch TV	
	2 slices of wholewheat toast	10-11 pm: read up on work	

Late night snack: 12 am	Popcorn: 1 bowl. Jasmine tea	11-12 pm : watch TV, have snack	
		1 am: to bed with a book	

Day 2

Breakfast: 10 am	Lemon tea with Splenda	9.30 am: wake up	Workout: 6-7 pm
	Sliced papaya	10-11.30 am: read papers, check mail, etc	
	5 almonds soaked overnight	12 noon: shower and get dressed	Cross-trainer: 30 mins
Snack: 12.30 pm	Brazil nuts: 10-12 pieces	12.15-1.30 pm: work on column	Cycle: 10 mins
Cold coffee: 1 pm	1 Barista cold coffee with sugar free	1.45-3.15 pm: meeting at work	Pilates: 20 mins
Lunch: 3.30 pm	Crostini with tomato	3.30 pm: lunch at Italian café	
	Salad with cheese	4-5.30 pm: Italian class at centre	

Snack: 7.30 pm	Diet Coke and roasted nuts: 1 bowl	6-7 pm: workout at gym	
Dinner: 10.30 pm	Bean and pasta soup: 1 bowl	7.30-8.30 pm: working on computer	
	Steak, vegetables and fries (10)	9 pm: dinner with friends	
	Champagne: 2 glasses	9.20-10.20 pm: drinks	
	Red wine: 2 glasses	10.30 pm: dinner	
Tea: 12 am	Jasmine tea: 4 cups	12 am: back home, jasmine tea and TV	
		12.30 am: read book in bed	
		1 am: to bed	

Day 3			
Tea: 8 am	1 cup tea, 2 Good Day biscuits	8-9 am: read newspapers in bed.	No workout
Breakfast: 9 am	2 rotis (1 lightly buttered), glass of milk with coffee and no sugar	9.30 am: Got ready for work	
		10.30 am: Went to Connaught Place to buy gifts, went to office, worked till 1.30 pm.	
Lunch: 1.30-2.30 pm	Cold coffee with sugar, ½ bowl of green vegetable salad with feta, half of a thin-crust, 6-inch vegetarian pizza.	Went out for lunch with friends to Khan Market.	
Tea: 5 pm	½ cup with no sugar	Reached home, worked for 2 hours on a story.	
Dinner: 7 pm	2 plain rotis, 1 piece chicken		

8.30- 10.30 pm	1 large vodka with soda and lime juice, 1½ shammi kababs, 5 pieces of roasted potatoes, cucumber, paneer and tomatoes in a veg chaat, 3 pieces of egg on toast (each piece 1/4th of a slice, fried, with scrambled egg on top).	Went out to meet some friends	
12.00- 12.30 pm		Read in bed.	
		Smoked 10-15 cigarettes	

Subject

This is the type of profile that I feel most sorry for. The recall belongs to what I call a 'thinker' (someone whose job involves a lot of intellectual work) with a sedentary lifestyle, who is making serious (and repeated) attempts to eat correctly and to commit to a regular exercise routine (sugar is out, sweetener is in). Rohini has been to every dietician you can name and has been on the 'lose and gain much more' cycle forever. Though she is very intellectual, what she is missing here is a basic awareness about what her body needs and at what times during the day.

Evaluation of the recall

The current diet is a cocktail of many diets that Rohini has tried, tested and given up. What she has retained (other than body fat and stretch marks) is various things from various diets that suited her palette and lifestyle. Except for one meal there is hardly anything fried or sweet.

Before we go on, I want to remind you again of the 4 basic principles that you need to employ to remain healthy and lean.

1. **Always eat the minute you wake up: never start your day with tea or coffee.**
2. **Eat every 2 to 3 hours during the day.**
3. **Eating (quantity of food) should be directly proportionate to your activity levels.**
4. **There should be a minimum gap of 2 hours between the last meal and bedtime.**

Now look at the recall. None of our principles are being followed. You can expect Rohini to look bloated and have a stomach which doesn't function too well. How can it? Dinner is usually big and late. She drinks too much chai in the morning. So what if it's jasmine, or decaf?

The most harmful things Rohini is doing:

- Not 1 or 2 but 4 cups of tea in the morning
- Starving till late afternoon and binging in the night. Rohini is a classic case of 'I can eat almost nothing till lunch and after that I am ravenous'—which applies to all those who refuse to feed themselves well in the day, either because they want to become diet divas, or have forgotten, or are too busy to eat.
- Rohini may not be eating much till evening, yet a lot of her activities like Italian class, meetings, checking emails, etc, get done by 6 to 7pm.
- To make things worse, she goes for a workout on an already ill-fed body and then eats nothing after workouts. Just look at what she is drinking pre exercise—Diet Coke! Come on ya.
- This can also lead to injuries. Your doc will deduce that working out at the gym injured you. It's like your mechanic saying, 'Gaadi road pe chalaya isliye kharab hua!' Use your common sense, if you drive your car without petrol, wo band pad jayegi!

My take

Rohini will look and feel dramatically different if she just changes the timings and how much she eats at one time. She can modify her diet as:

Meal 1 (9.30 am): bowl of papaya
Meal 2 (10.30 am): muesli, milk and nuts
Meal 3 (12.30-1 pm): grilled chicken with 2 pieces of wholewheat toast
Meal 4 (2.30-3 pm): slice of cheese
Meal 5 (5-5.30 pm): Brazil nuts
Meal 6 (7-7.30 pm): bean and pasta soup (post workout)
Meal 7 (9 pm): roasted peppers and other veggies, plus grilled fish if she wants to

Profile 2: Lubna, 28 years old, banker

Day 1 Holiday			
Food/ Drink	Quantity	Activity Recall	Workout
		12:30 pm: went out for shopping	
Lunch: 3 pm	1 plate of rice with chicken curry, fish and salad and pickle	2-3 pm: watched TV	
		3 pm: had lunch	
Tea: 5.30 pm	Tea with bread and butter and kheer	3.30-5 pm: nap	
		5.30 pm: had tea	
Dinner: 9.30 pm	1 plate of chicken biryani and ice cream	6-10 pm: went out to cousin's place for dinner	
		11 pm: had shower	
		12 pm: went to sleep	

Day 2			
		6.20 am: woke up and got ready	Nothing
Breakfast: 7.15-7.25 am	1 bowl of cornflakes and 1 cup of tea	7.30 am: left for work	
		Work timings: 7.45 am-4 pm	
		4.45 pm: Reach home	
Lunch: 12 pm	1 sandwich, salad and mutton curry	07.30-10 pm: was in church for mass	
Snack: 2 pm	Fruits (I only eat this when I have the time)	10.30 pm: reached home and watched cricket match	
Tea: 4.45 pm	Tea with biscuits and cake	11.00 pm: showered	
		11.30 pm: dinner with family	
Dinner: 11.30 pm	1 plate of rice with fried fish, salad	12.00 am: bedtime	

Day 3			
Breakfast: 7.15-7.25 am	1 bowl of porridge and 1 cup of tea	6.20 am: woke up and got ready	Nothing
		7.30 am: left for work	
		Work timings: 7.45 am-4 pm	
At work	I have at least 2 to 3 glasses of water when I have time in the office.	4.45 pm: reached home	
Lunch: 12.00 noon	1 chapati with beef roast	5.30-7 pm: watched TV and talked with family	
Snack: 2.00 pm	1 mango	7-10.30 pm: went out with family to the mall	
	½ cup aloo sabzi	11pm: had shower	
4.45 pm	1 plate of rice with curry fish, beef roast and plain raw mango	11.30 pm: had dinner with family	

Tea: 6.00 pm	Had tea with icing cake	12.30 pm: bedtime	
Dinner: 11.30 pm	1 plate of foul medammes (Lebanese dish of beans) with bread and fish curry. Later 1 banana.		

Subject

Lubna is from (where else, but) Kerala and currently living in the Middle East. A young girl of 28, she holds a good job with a bank (sorry, not as a nurse). She lives with her extended family but misses her immediate family. When in Kerala, Lubna ate much more than she eats now. But she never gained any weight. She had lustrous hair, glowing skin and regular periods. Three years away from home and she had gained 28 kilos! She never realised she was gaining weight, she was too busy managing her life and living alone in a new country. The lustre from her hair, the glow from her face, her confidence and the regularity of her periods had gone.

Evaluation of the recall

Now, this girl believes she's unnecessarily gaining weight. She thinks her diet is rich in lean proteins like fish and chicken and that she rarely has sweets.

This is totally untrue if you look at her recall, she eats ice cream and kheer on day 1 and cakes on the remaining days! But of course she is gaining weight because she is just so unaware of what she is doing. She has tried exercising and given up because 'It doesn't work anyways.'

The most harmful things she is doing:

- Not exercising. First things first, she needs to commit to some kind of exercise at least 3 to 4 days a week.
- Lubna mostly eats chicken and fish, which is alright, but if it comes so late in the day then it just gets converted to fat because the body is really in no mood to digest and assimilate chicken and ice cream or fish and banana!
- She does follow our principle of not waking up to tea or coffee but then doing anything in isolation is never enough. Here is the reason why she went on a diet with me.

Dear Ms Rujuta Diwekar,
Hi, my name is Lubna. I live in Dubai and am a big fan of Kareena Kapoor. I simply love her. And in Jab We Met *she is sooo cute.*
I want to thank you for two things:
For making Kareena Kapoor so thin and sexy and also for helping me lose weight.
While researching on the internet I found out that Kareena is following your diet and doesn't have tea or coffee as the first thing in the morning. I idolise her

*and want to look like her so I stopped having bed tea.
The result—I lost 5 kilos in 2 months. But now my
weight is stuck. Can you help me please?*

As with Rohini, Lubna doesn't follow the 2nd, 3rd
or the 4th principle. While she is at work she barely
eats. After coming back home she hogs. Yet she
believes that she is eating right.

Now if you are wondering why she lost weight
after quitting her chai as the wake up drink, here
is the simple reason: it put her in touch with her
hunger. So she started having breakfast, which
helped to improve her metabolic rate.

My take

Now look at why she is gaining weight. This
girl simply eats too much. But why? When she
comes back from work she has nothing creative or
interesting to do. She hasn't bothered cultivating any
hobby or working out. So she is eating sweets for
entertainment. (All girls do that and that makes them
put on weight.) Interestingly, on the day that she goes
to church there is no dessert in the night. Prayers are
comforting. When you are already feeling happy with
yourself you can do away with 'comfort food'.

**Eating food for entertainment is a sure shot way
of getting fat.** It's a much better idea to take
part in some activity that is comforting. Praying,
exercising, painting, singing, anything that suits

your temperament. It doesn't just help you burn calories, it keeps you away from ingesting too many calories. Food is not for entertainment or to deal with boredom. Look at Lubna's diet recall. The girl consumes huge amounts of food at a time. One way of getting over boredom is to eat till your senses go numb. So along with changing her eating habits and exercising 3 times a week, Lubna will also need to cultivate hobbies so that she can utilise her spare time better. She can modify her diet as:

Meal 1 (6.30 am): Mango
Meal 2 (7.30 am): Porridge
Meal 3 (9.30 am): 1 chapati with omelette (roll and wrap in aluminium foil)
Meal 4 (11.30 am): yogurt
Meal 5 (1.30 pm): 1 chapati and bhaji
Meal 6 (3.30 pm): a handful of nuts
Meal 7 (5 pm): 1 chapati and sabzi (after getting back from work)
Get some exercise or join some class—do something productive by 6-6.30 pm.
Meal 8 (7.30 pm): brown rice, dal and fish (steamed or as curry)

Bedtime should be earlier by 10 to 10.30 pm, as Lubna gets up by 6 to 6.30 am. Good rest ensures that the body functions at its best and prevents frequent illnesses. (Lubna used to fall sick frequently, nothing serious but backaches, flus, coughs, colds, etc. Basically, poor immunity.)

Profile 3: Aditi, working mom, early 30s

	Day 1		
Food/ drink	Quantity	Activity recall	Workout
			Yoga for an hour
	8 oz glass of warm water with ½ lemon	7 am: woke up and started preparing lunch for my son.	
Breakfast: 8.35-8.50 am	8 oz glass of whole milk with elaichi powder and some kesar (no sugar).	7.25-8 am: got my son and myself ready and a glass of milk.	
		8-8.30 am: left to work and dropped my son to school by car.	
10.30 am	20 oz of Diet Pepsi.	8.45 am: reached office and started working.	
	8 oz of low fat yogurt.		
11.15 am- 12.15 pm		Yoga class	
Lunch: 12.30 pm	Small veggie sandwich from Quiznos. Sandwich was on wheat sub bread with lettuce, 2 slices of cheese, 2 slices of tomato, couple of black olives, onions and mushrooms.		

1- 4.30 pm		Got back to work on computer (Business software analyst).	
4.30-5 pm		Picked up my son and drove towards home.	
5.20 pm		Reached home. Started cooking dinner .	
Dinner: 6.30 pm	2 plain rotis (no butter or ghee), 2 bowls of french bean subji with eggplant.	Had dinner	
6.30-7.30 pm		Fed my son. Cleaned the dishes and kitchen.	
7.30-9.30 pm		Relaxed with my son and watched some TV.	
10 pm		Went to bed. Woke up couple of times a night as son was sick.	

		Day 2		
	8 oz glass of warm water with lemon.	7 am: woke up	
7-7.30 am		Prepared lunch and packed for my son.	
7.30-8 am		Got myself and son ready.	
8-8.45 am		Dropped son to school and reached work.	
Breakfast: 9 am	3 egg omlette with vegetables and 2 slices of cheese in the downstairs deli.	Had breakfast	
11 am	20 oz of Diet Coke		
11.30-1 pm		Had a hair cut appointment. Skipped lunch grabbed some fresh fruit on the way.	
Lunch: 1-2.30 pm	Watermelon, pineapple, strawberry and some grapes.	Had fruits in the meeting. Meeting lasted till 2.30 pm.	
2.30-3.15 pm		Went for a walk with a colleague in the office campus.	Stroll with a friend.
3.15-5.30 pm		Worked on computers again.	

5.30-6 pm		Picked up son and went to a restaurant close by as was starving.	
Dinner: 6-7.30 pm	Had 1 dish of dahi puri (5 puris) and 1 plate of pav bhaji	Had dinner and spend some quality family time.	
8 pm		Reached home.	
8-8.30 pm		Freshen up, helped son to fresh up.	
8.30-9.30 pm		Exercise	Walked on treadmill for an hour at the speed of 3.5 km/ hr with 0 incline.
9.30-10 pm		Storytime for my son.	
10.30 pm		Went to sleep. Woke up couple of times at night as son still has congetion and wakes up middle of the night for water.	

Day 3			
Morning		6.30 am: woke up.	
6.30-7.30 am		Prepared lunch snacks for son and packed for school.	
7.30-8 am		Got son ready and all 3 of us left for work and school.	
8-8.30 am		Reached work after dropping son.	
Breakfast: 9 am	8 oz of yogurt.		
9-11.15 am		Worked on computers; drank 20 oz of water bottle.	
11.15-12.15 pm		Pilates class	
Lunch: 12.30-1 pm	Plain rawa dosa with sambhar and coconut chutney	Lunch at a south Indian restaurant	
1-5 pm		Worked on computers again; drank another 20 oz of water.	
5-5.30 pm		Picked up Aditya from school.	
6.00 pm		Reached home and started cooking.	

Dinner: 6.45 pm	Potato-brinjal mix vegetable with 2 parathas (I try to do my parathas as thin as possible so I feel I am eating 2 parathas although I am eating the equivalent of 1)	Had dinner.	
7-7.30 pm		Fed dinner to Aditya.	
7.30-8.30 pm		Played toys with him.	
8.30-10 pm		Storytime for him; drank another 30 oz of water.	
10 pm		Went to sleep.	

Subject

Aditi is a sharp girl from India who first went to study to America on scholarship and later worked, married and had her bundle of joy, Aditya, there. So what goes without saying is that other than parents and in-laws being around for the customary 6-9 months post delivery, she has had little or no help around the house. Indians abroad, especially women, get a really raw deal. No family around, worse no maids! And when you have a mind that's conditioned the Indian way, you are almost always feeling that no matter how well you do at work your self worth depends on how well you do as a mother, wife, homemaker, sister, daughter, daughter-in-law, friend, etc (though not necessarily in that order). Actually all of us women world over, caste, creed, nationality, IQ, and financial security aside feel like that. (Wah, what a leveller!) Women, after bearing children and especially a son, happily give up themselves and their identities for the second time. (They give it up the first time when they become somebody's Mrs.)

From Mrs Aggarwal she becomes Bunty ki mummy. Oh what a transformation. Once upon a time women were not expected to be computer savvy, professional working women. They were supposed to make chapatis, cook, clean, etc. Today they are expected to look hot, care for their children, cook, clean, make presentations, crack deals... the list is endless. In short, to make money and chapatis with equal ease. This expectation comes from the women themselves.

Evaluation of the recall

Look at this diet recall. What does Aditi do for herself? Nothing at all. Does she even exist? Not really. She wakes up for her son, cooks for him, and looks good so that she is 'presentable in office'. She has never lost the weight she gained during pregnancy (sounds familiar na?). She doesn't seem to think of herself from the moment she wakes up till the time she goes to bed, and even after she goes to bed. So she wakes up at 7 am but doesn't eat a thing for the next 1 to 2 hours. She prepares lunch but doesn't even have the time to grab a fruit or coffee (though I disapprove of coffee). She understands that eating is important, and that's exactly why she cooks a healthy meal for her son every day even if she has had a disturbed sleep the night before. Now all that she needs to do is extend this understanding towards herself.

If you look at her activity, she does quite a bit, cooks, drives, works, works out, but she doesn't really love herself enough so she barely feeds herself. Makes a real effort to eat light; Diet Pepsi, light wheat sandwich, fruits, etc. But in the process of eating light she is almost starving herself. Now when we eat too little and when the gap between our meals are big, like Aditi's, our body learns to store fat.

My take

Aditi is frustrated and you can see this in the fact that she isn't up to exercise, or anything else for that matter. She is a great mom to Aditya but all her energies are getting consumed with routine activities at home and work. She tries hard to eat right but there are no 'results'. When she does freak out on food, like the day she ate pav bhaji and pani puri, she punishes herself by excercising; in this case walking for an hour on the treadmill. Exercise is not meant as punishment for the body. Not for getting fat or overeating or anything else. Exercise is a way to improve fitness, blood circulation, and to love the body. If it's used for anything else, or if it's abused, it stops working.

The good part about Aditi's diet recall is that she follows principle 4 and has an early dinner. But on days that she places more demands on her body and mind, like staying up if her son is sick, or exercises, she needs to up her daily intake of food.

Aditi can make the following changes to her diet based on what we have learned in the book:

Meal 1 (7 am): 1 Banana (easy to eat and won't take time away from cooking for the son)

Meal 2 (8-8.30 am): 2 egg white omelette with 2 slices of wholewheat bread (can be eaten at home or carried to work in case she's short on time)

Meal 3 (10-10.30 am): a handful of peanuts (can be stored in office)

Meal 4 (12.30-1 pm): veggie sandwich or idli/dosa or carry snack that has been cooked for son

Meal 5 (3-3.30 pm): bowl of curd or fruit yogurt (can be stored at work)

Meal 6 (5-5.30 pm): soy milk or skim milk

Meal 7 (7 pm): 2 chapatis or parathas and sabzi (the way Aditi makes them—thin)

Meal 8: glass of skim milk with elaichi (if up till late or active)

Profile 4: Atul Naik, businessman, late 40s

Day / Time	Tuesday	Wednesday	Thursday
6 am	Wake up	Wake up	1 banana
7 am	1 cup tea and 2 biscuits (Parle Glucose)		1 cup tea and 2 biscuits (Nice)
8 am		1 cup tea and 5 Nice biscuits	
9 am	2 slices bread with butter	1 fried egg	Bhurji
10 am	Leave for work	Leave for work	Leave for work
11 am			
12 pm			
Lunch: 1 pm	4 chapatis, rice, dal, vegetable and 1 vati dahi.	4 chapatis, rice, dal, vegetable and 1 vati dahi.	Noodles, chowmein, American chopsuey, honey with noodles
2 pm			
Snack: 3 pm	1 apple	1 apple	Pint of beer
4 pm			
5 pm			
6 pm			

7 pm	50 grams fried namkeens	50 grams fried namkeens	
8 pm			
Dinner: 9 pm	4 chapatis, rice, dal, vegetables	6 chapatis with brinjal and potato bhaji	Instant noodles— made by Ahana

Time	Activity
06.00	Wake up
07.00	Bathroom
	Newspapers
08.00	Calls, etc
09.00	
10.00	Leave for work
11.00	At it. On phone, email, etc
12.00	All sedentary work
14.00	Meeting or some boring
	conference
15.00	
16.00	Back to serious work
17.00	
18.00	Leave from work
19.00	Reach home and watch TV
20.00	TV, email and spend time with the girls
21.00	Dinner

Subject

The profile belongs to a successful entrepreneur who is an IIT graduate with an MBA from America. It's a typical profile of a highly successful, intelligent and easygoing personality. Atul Naik, blessed with a high metabolic rate, ate everything he could lay his hands on while he lived on the IIT campus in Mumbai. The story was similar when he lived a student's life in America for a couple of years, and then worked, as a bachelor.

As an IIT student, he, along with his batchmates had cycled from Mumbai to Kanyakumari (which to date is his favourite memory) and he has gone on many a youth hostel trek in the Himalaya. His love and passion for exercise continued in the US, and he took part in the Boston Marathon, skiing in Chicago, etc. Back in Mumbai, his love for exercise prevailed but there were no avenues for outdoor training in Aamchi Mumbai. So several years passed, and Atul married and had 2 gorgeous daughters. Though he now ran his own company, with over 400 employees, he continued to lead a student's life at least as far as diet is concerned.

Exercise disappeared from the daily menu. But on every holiday there would be a sporadic period of activity or day of snorkelling, rappelling, trekking, etc. And he was always amongst the best. He never failed to show how 'fit' he was to his daughters, but then one day his daughters told him that his prowess didn't mean a thing if he still retained his paunch. 'Look at Shah Rukh Khan in "Dard-e-Disco"! So sexy... so lean and mean,' they said, 'Dad, at least when we hug you our fingers should touch each other.'

Atul was up for the bet. He was jealous that his girls thought the world of Shah Rukh Khan just because of his 'stupid dard-e-disco dance'.

Evaluating the recall

Look at his recall. Breakfast is chai with biscuits. Lunch and dinner is very big. Also, he is one of those rare species in Mumbai which gets home by 6.30 to 7 pm. But instead of heading straight for dinner, he prefers eating junk (that's also the time he is hungry the most) and then eats dinner at 9 to 9.30 pm while watching his favourite TV show. Today, our student-at-heart is over 40 years old. And at one of his executive checkups, he was surprised to see he was borderline everything: diabetes, cholesterol, triglycerides, BP, etc. With a diet that had remained unchanged for years (after 10th standard), he wondered why he was a borderline case now. But though the diet had stayed pretty much the same, activity had dramatically changed and come down to almost zero. From taking a bus everywhere and walking the remaining distance (if short of money) and 15 to 20 days of trekking or cycling once every year; to being driven to the doorstep of his home and office every day and holidaying abroad twice every year (where other than one day of activity, the rest was beer and chilling, sightseeing at best), Atul had come a long way. So had his waist.

He joined the Marathon Programme I run: it was finally an outdoor activity in Mumbai, and IITians love the structured training that I offer. However, Atul thought he could eat whatever he wanted now that he was exercising, and results would follow. With no change in diet the 'results' didn't come but he got better and better at running, felt stronger and much more flexible than before. Atul's sense of wellbeing improved but the size of his waist didn't decrease (marginally yes, but compared to how fit he felt, it was nothing). Now that's the best thing about exercise. Our body is blessed with 'muscle memory'. So if you have a high amount of accumulated fitness time or if you have been regularly exercising 20 to 30 years ago, you will quickly recover your fitness levels to what they used to be before you quit working out. (That's exactly why I tell my clients that not even a minute you spend exercising is wasted. Our body carries that samskara or impression forever. So if you can exercise only once a month, go ahead and even do that to start with; you'll help your body accumulate fitness memory.)

My take

Now, for people like Atul Naik, who are high on ability and low on discipline and motivation, following a diet is the biggest challenge (they are also a nutritionist's worst nightmare). This category has already made excuses for not following a diet: too many client meetings, too many work commitments, too much travel, no support from wife, etc. But the best part is that if they watch their diet, they get results the fastest. Atul Naik can modify his diet like this:

Meal 1 (6 am): banana
Meal 2 (8 am): 2 chapatis and 2 to 3 egg white bhurji or omelette
Meal 3 (10 am): a slice of cheese (stored in office or car)
Meal 4 (noon): 3 chapatis, dal and sabzi
Meal 5 (2-3 pm): rice and dahi
Meal 6 (5-5.30 pm): idli, dosa or sandwich from office canteen
Meal 7 (7.30 pm): 2 chapatis; fish, chicken or sabzi

Profile 5: On a break to lose weight1

Sunday	Note: I am on leave till June end, hence do not have much office work these days but attending lot of meetings		
Early morning	Ate 1 banana before going to Walkeshwar with 1 spoon chawanprash	5.45 am woke up and fresh up/brush	Went to Walkeshwar with Ruchita, run entire hill of Hanging Garden (approx 4.6 kilometres)
	Ate 1 banana after the run		
Breakfast: 9.05-9.15 am	8.30 am had 1 glass of watermelon juice. 9 am had 1 cup tea with 1 khakhra (roasted chapati)	8.00 am return and read newspapers, relax till 9.00 am	
	Had some namkeen also	10.00 am went to temple	
		11.00 am, went to VT to bring mango juice and some ice cream as we were expecting many guests at our house for lunch.	

12.30 pm	1 glass of watermelon juice		
Drinks and some namkeen before lunch: 1.30 pm	2 pegs of Irish baileys with some cashewnuts and wafers and some salads	Met all the guests and had chit chats	
Lunch: 2.30 pm	2 katori dal, 3 roti, 2 bowl of mango juice, 2 bowl of boondi raita, 1 katori gattanu sak (vegetable), 4 pieces of dhokala	Entertained guests at our house for lunch, chit chat and general discussion till 7.00 pm	
Tea: 5.00 pm	1 cup tea		
		7.30 pm, went to pick-up Ishita from her classes	
Dinner: 8.30 pm	2 pav with 1 katori 'bhaji', some sweets	9 pm read e-mails	
	2 bowls of mango Juice	9.30-11.00 pm watched cricket match on TV	
		11.30 pm slept	

Monday	Note : Every Thursday and Saturday, I fast, which means I take either lunch or dinner and liquid and friuts, dry fruits		
	Ate 1 banana before going to gym with 1 spoon chawanprash	Got up at 6.30, went to drop Ishita for her volleyball classes	
		7.30 am went to gym	30 minutes of cycling and some gym activity, 200 times skipping
Breakfast: 8.45-9.15 am	1 cup tea and 2 khakhara and 1 plate watermelon	8.30 am return and read newspapers relax till 9.00 am	
	Some namkeen	9.00 am breakfast	
		Drop daughter to classes at 10.30 am; picked her up at 12.30 am	
	Ate 2 angir at 12 noon at sister's house	11-11.30 am attended a meeting. Then went to sister's house till 12.15 pm	
		Picked up the younger one from class	

219

Lunch: 1.30 pm	2 bowls rice and 1 glass of buttermilk, 1 glass mango juice and 1 plate thokala	
		2-4.30 am slept, watched *CNBC*, read books
		4.30 pm went to drop elder one to class.
Tea: 5.00 pm	1 cup tea	5-6 am spoke to some friends over phone
		6 pm went to meet Ruchita/ Tejal
	8 am had a lot of watermelon before dinner	
Dinner: 9.00 pm	1 plate panipuri, 1 burger, 1 frankie and 2 pieces of grilled sandwiches	Went out with friends for dinner at 9 pm
		9.30-11 pm watched cricket match on TV
		12.00 pm slept

Tuesday			
	Ate 1 banana before going to gym with 1 spoon chawanprash	Got up at 6.30, went to drop Ishita for her volleyball classes	
		7.30 am went to gym	45 minutes ST training under Ali at Ruia College Gym
Breakfast: 8.45 am	1 plate idli/vada/sambhar and 1 tea at Manish's restaurant	9.30 return home with Ishita	
		10.30 went to drop younger one to classes	
		11 am till 1 pm attended meetings	
Lunch: 1.30 pm	3 chapati/1 bowl of vegetable/1 mango/2 bowls of kadhi and some rice and papads and 2 pieces of sweets	Again heavy lunch	
		3.30 to 6.00 slept, watched *CNBC*	

Tea: 6.00 pm	1 cup tea with some namkeen	6.00-7.30 read books	
1 mango at 7.30 pm		7.30-8 pm pranayam yoga	
Dinner: 9.30 pm	1 plate dhokala and 2 chapatis with mango	Watched cricket match till 11.30 pm	
		slept at 11.30 midnight	

Subject

Jayesh is taking a break in between jobs. His earlier job was extremely high profile. The next one is going to be even bigger. But he has taken the break of 1 month in between because he felt he was losing out on who he was as a person. He wanted to be much more in contact with his children, know where and what time they went for their various activities, attend their PTA meetings, get to know their friends, meet up with his own friends and family, and of course start exercising. His big aim was to lose weight while he was off work. Work involved a lot of travelling, and he had happily assumed that if you were travelling to a different continent every fortnight you couldn't lose weight.

Evaluating the recall

Our man Jayesh is a true Gujju bhai. He loves his mangoes and loves variety for dinner. (Craving variety for dinner is a condition that grips the Gujurati, Jain and Kacchi community. They believe that eating anything other than rice, roti, vegetable, dal or kadhi for dinner is variety. Basically variety means eating all the junk in the world. It wins brownie points with in-laws and children demand it like their birthright. The women in these communities are always fooling themselves by saying things like: 'Pizza banaya but wholewheat base tha, panipuri mein moong sprouts dala, pav bhaji ka bread brown tha, dhokla ke vagaar mein sirf 2 teaspoon oil dala, wo bhi olive.')

All that this 'variety' does is increases the size of women's hips and men's waists. Jayesh, a level headed banker, was really disturbed when I told him that he couldn't be eating panipuri (our beloved Mumbai version of the golgappa).

'Why?' he asked, 'It's so healthy its just water and sprouts.'

'Yes, but it's all in a deep-fried puri,' I said. But he just ignored me.

Now, if you look at his profile you notice that he is not waking up to tea or coffee, which is great. But the gaps in his meals are big, especially between lunch and dinner. We need to inculcate the habit of eating frequently into his schedule. We have long gaps in meals when we travel and we have them when we are at home too. So it's not about how accessible food is to you. It's about whether you have learnt to get in touch with your hunger signals and learnt to feed your body.

When Jayesh travelled and cracked deals, his reason to not eat anything were: I'm in transit, in meeting, in conference, nothing vegetarian available, etc. But what's the reason for big gaps when at home? Nothing, other than no training to eat frequently. So, he is not following our eat every 2 to 3 hours principle.

Nor is he following our principle 3, that eating is directly proportionate to activity. His meals in the morning when he is exercising are small, and the size and calories of the meals go up as the day progresses, while his activities start going down. (So, an inverse ratio!)

He does have a gap of 2 hours between dinner and bedtime, but his dinners are big and full of variety so they don't provide any nourishment, only calories. Apart from this, Jayesh is bang on with his plan. Dropping off and picking up his children, taking his wife out to breakfast places, exercising in the morning and chilling out in the afternoon and evenings.

My take

What he now needs to do is eat better in the mornings because he is exercising in the morning, reduce the size of his lunch and dinners, and eat much more frequently. Also, he needs to treat mango like the fruit it is. The way an orange, apple or pineapple is treated. Which means that it can't be a part of his meals. It will have to be consumed solo, like any other fruit.

Mangoes and potatoes are 2 food items with an unnecessarily tainted reputation. But it's what we do with mangoes and potatoes that makes them fattening. Consuming deep-fried potatoes will surely make us fat. But deep frying anything, even oranges, will make us fat.

Mangoes are eaten as if they are a sweet dish, instead of a fruit. Mango juice is eaten with puris and chapatis. And because we all love the way chapati and aamras tastes, we have an extra chapati. It's this eating pattern which makes us fat, not the fruit. And anyways, it's always a better idea to eat the whole fruit instead of its juice. Would you ever have puri with watermelon juice? No. Then stop having it with mango juice.

Some simple things are going to help Jayesh:

Meal 1 (6.30 am): banana and chawanprash
Meal 2 (8.30 am): mango
Meal 3 (10 am): idli, dosa or upma
Meal 4 (Noon): 2 to 3 rotis or brown rice, sabzi and dal
Meal 5 (2.30-3 pm): dahi and salad
Meal 6 (5-6 pm): dhokla/khakra
Meal 7 (8 pm): 1-2 rotis, kadhi and sabzi

When I work with people on their diets, firstly I encourage them to make changes based on what they understand about their diet and activity recall, and on the 4 common sense diet principles. It's only after they follow a basic healthy diet for a while that I start tweaking and fine-tuning it. I see my role more as an educator than as a crutch. Basic understanding of your own life pattern, activity and hunger signals is imperative. No nutritionist or the fees they charge can substitute for this. The only way to stay lean and healthy for life is to develop a strong understanding about your nutrient needs, and to stay connected with your gut at all times. In fact 'gut feeling' is what I wanted to call my book. But my editor (smart girl) wanted to connect with the audience hence those words: lose weight. This grabs eyeballs.

Most of my clients go through a slow, progressive change. What changes is something deep within. This change is brought about by developing awareness about how, what and when we eat or don't eat, can affect the way we think and look. So the ice cream, kaju katri, alcohol, etc is still there but your response to it changes.

This is also a reason why I am a non believer in before and after pictures. What changes after developing awareness cannot be photographed and is not visible to the physical eye. It can only be experienced.

Now, here's a little excerpt from the diet diary of one of my clients Shabnam. If I were to give her profile a name I would call it: 'finding myself after marriage'. (Early marriage and 8 kilos gained within 2 years of being married.)

So,
I can't believe it, almost 3 weeks are up and yes there is a change.
Visible changes in inches:
Chest: Previous: 39.8 Now: 39.3
Hips: Previous: 45.5 Now: 44.4
Tummy: has also gone in... but I don't remember my previous measurement... so not comparing it.
Overall: again, very happy... No bloating... water intake is still between 3 to 4 litres (was wondering if so much water washes minerals away?)
Major change: I have developed a sense of very good self control. I can say no... and feel happy about my decision and actually not desire the particular food... , in fact be quite repulsed by it... I want to eat only what I want to eat (ie what you give me to eat)... I go out of my way, even if it looks absurd... cook every day, grocery shop every day, work around my meals so carefully, that I can't give myself an excuse that, 'Oh you know I did not have time, and the cook forgot to buy the particular thing so I just ate something else'.
I plan my diet every day in advance, and I spend so much of my time to ensure that I am eating and drinking water. And even if I have to go out, I consciously order what I need to eat, and not more

and not less. And I do not even sneak a bite here and there.

Even when people around me are forcing to just take one lick of their ice cream, I do a tiny fake lick, and say I don't like it AND I ACTUALLY DON'T (which is the best part). So I am more confident of myself that even when I have to eat out, I don't go crazy and binge. I look for the BEST alternative to my meal plan... and am happy and satisfied eating that. Wow... this is a major change!

Also, as discussed over phone, my metabolic rate seems to be on the move. I am full after breakfast (thanks to the yummy hearty one), find myself getting full easily at lunch... and starving within 2 hours... just before my fruit/yogurt time.

The cheese snack, after fruit, doesn't satisfy me, and I feel like having nariyal pani... or coffee... or something else to fill me.

But post that, and right after workout, not hungry any more... and when I am eating dinner, I am not starving at dinner time... I am eating because I know I need to eat...

So I guess its a good sign that I am most hungry till 4.30-5 pm... and then my hunger reduces as the sun sets... !☺ You are like some magician, eh?☺

Alright, attached is my diary... and going to continue my zig zag diet...

Next week is going to be a tough week...

My dad is flying in from Dubai. He and my mom are the only two people who know that I am doing this diet with you and are super happy and proud of me. (*I am convincing my mom to join you as well.*☺) *He is coming on Tuesday and leaving on Friday evening. I said we can only do one meal out, I will use that as my bi-weekly cheat meal (that again is on your approval).*

And I have to go on a dinner on Monday, at family friends.☹ *It is my soup and stir fry day... so I guess I will do soup at home... and nibble on some home cooked veggies there... and salad... it is the same people who I went for dinner with on Wednesday, and faked a tummy ache...*

So I will just continue on the streak... I am being light at night nowadays...

Talk to you soon

Luv

Shabbo

6

Crossing the bridge: from knowing to doing

Ok, now that we have collected all the gyan, we need to put it together to make it of some real use for us. Without it, this book too will become like everything else we already know about diet and exercise: impotent information that will never bear the fruit of health, well-being, and peace.

Just knowing or talking about things like eating right and exercising regularly has never helped anybody. 'Just talking is not enough,' said the people of Mumbai to its politicians after the terror attacks on CST, Taj, Oberoi, Leopold and Nariman House. Our government has been talking for way too long, and doing precious little. No wonder then that our country continues to remain a soft target for the terrorists. They come and attack us almost like making a style statement to the world: 'Hey we are alive and kicking and can strike at will.'

Isn't this situation similar to what we do to our bodies. Talk and yak-yak-yak (just like a Ladakhi souvenir T-shirt) about dieting, exercise and do absolutely nothing about it. No wonder then that our stomach continues to be a soft target. And at the same time we want our stomachs to have the 'resilient spirit of Mumbai', which means that it should continue to function just as well. 'Chalta hai' is the beej mantra here. Do your work well, my dear stomach. So what if I stuff so much food inside you that you feel like an overcrowded Virar local?

Are we going to do the same thing to our digestive system that we hate our politicians for? Enough of taking our bodies for granted. Let's not push our stomachs to revolt against us. Let's take some real action. And like one of the placards in the peace march in Mumbai declared: 'We are against terrorists not against Pakistan', it's important that the action that we take is not misplaced. Food, sanitation and education for all, is probably the most fundamental step to tackling terrorism. (Shah Rukh Khan once said that if he was the prime minister for a day he would build toilets all over so that women and the poor would not go through daily humiliation.)

So what are the fundamental steps towards adopting a healthier lifestyle? Here goes.

Step 1

Wake up closer to sunrise.

Ideally: wake up a little before sunrise so that you can witness the peace that every dawn brings. It's not called 'awakening' for nothing. Don't just leave this activity to when you are at hill stations. Dawn brings hope and energy for not just the day, but for life. Sunrise provides us with the vitamin D that we need to maintain healthy bones, gives us the 'me time' to clear our head, and cleanses our body of the tamas or the sloth of the night.

Let's get real: ok, sunrise is great. But if this sounds way out of reach, just wake up an hour before you are used to. If you are waking up post noon, start with waking up 2 hours earlier. Waking up even 30 minutes earlier gives us much needed time to workout, exercise.

Step 2

Eat within 10 minutes of waking up.

Ideally: eat meal 1 within 10 minutes of waking up. And obviously you can't start with tea, coffee or a cigarette. If you can't bring yourself to eat a big meal, start with a fruit. Absolutely any fruit is great. Keep it fresh, not frozen. Don't add salt, sugar, chaat masala, etc to it. And of course, don't squeeze it into a juice.

Let's get real: 10 minutes sounds like a big deal? Ok, eat within the first 30 minutes of waking up. But make sure that you are not reading your paper, checking your B-berry, giving instructions on the phone, etc while doing this. If you workout first thing on rising, eat a fruit before working out. And please don't eat in bed. Get up, walk around a bit, and then go for your food.

Step 3

Within an hour of meal 1, eat a nice, home cooked breakfast.

Ideally: a hot breakfast is the perfect meal 2 as it is freshly prepared and full of nutrients. Idli, dosa, uttapam, upma, parathas (cooked on the tawa but not fried), porridge, most egg dishes (scrambled, boiled, poached, omelettes) are good options. Breakfast is the meal that needs to become the family meal, instead of dinner. Eating early improves metabolic rate, arrests ageing, and reduces hunger pangs in the day.

Let's get real: family breakfast sounds straight out of a Sooraj Barjatya movie? Ok, so you have no time or facilities for a home cooked hot breakfast. Buy organic muesli from your local health store or just buy cereal which is not malted and hasn't had sugar added to it (look at the ingredients on the side of the box). To this, add some milk or yogurt and get going. And if you can only have breakfast on reaching office, try and eat something that is not deep-fried; many of us tend to pick up a samosa, bhaji, etc, something easily available. Try to take a homemade roll or sandwich with you, for example.

Notes
- This is also a good time for a multivitamin or a B vitamin supplement.

- On days that you are running late, skip meal 1 but make sure you have meal 2 before running out of the house.

Step 4

Eat every 2 hours after meal 2.

Ideally: calculate the number of hours that you spend away from home. Divide that by 2 and carry those many meals with you. So if you leave home at 8.30 am and return at 7 pm, you are out of the house for 10 and a half hours. You should then be eating 5 to 6 meals. For optimum fat burning, lunch should be around 11 am instead of the usual 1.30-2 pm. If you have the luxury of going home for lunch, do so. If not, wherever you are, sit in peace and eat. Avoid eating while standing, walking, or driving.

Let's get real: you are out for 12 hours and dividing this by 2 brings it to 6 meals! You can't possibly carry that much, and come on, you don't have boys to carry it around or staff to organise this like superstars do. But don't worry. Not all your meals have to be complicated. Most of you are used to bringing lunch to work. Eat that at 11 am as your meal 3. For all the in between meals, here are a few options that can easily be stacked in your office drawer; or your office boy can easily be instructed to buy for you. Some, like the poha, upma and vegetables, you can bring from home too.

1. Nariyal pani—and eat the malai.
2. Lassi without salt or sugar, but you can have other seasonings like jeera, dhaniya and pepper.
3. Channa and peanuts: easily stored at office. Just make sure your colleagues don't know where you store them or they will be over before you know. Or get your singdana wala to bring you a 5 rupee packet daily. Make sure you eat them without masala and avoid the deep-fried ones. Buy the ones that are roasted.
4. Cheese: buy a packet of singles or cubes. (Preferably cow cheese.) They can stay without refrigeration. Best kept out of others' sight. Great for keeping that glow on the face.
5. Curd or yogurt: there are many varieties available in the market and in various sizes. Take your pick. Great for digestion problems.
6. Milk or soy milk: get your regular dose of protein and fat. They are available in one time serving sizes and there are flavoured milk and soy milk options now.
7. Carrots or cucumbers: easy to carry. Won't leak like tomatoes. And remember, no need to peel or cut; just wash and eat for maximum enjoyment and nutrition.
8. Boiled eggs or omelettes: can be bought locally (usually near every office) or cooked in your office pantry, even. Or you can bring

the boiled egg in from home and keep it in its shell. It might smell though.

9. Protein bars: great-tasting and easy to store or carry (not to be confused with cereal bars, which are high in carbs). These are found in gyms, sports and health food stores.

10. Poha, upma, idlis, dosas, parathas or grilled sandwiches from a local eatery or pantry. So you eat only half of what you've got, share with your colleagues and earn brownie points with them.

11. Sprouts. Keep a sprout maker at work place. Refill it once every 2 days. And eat a handful of sprouts from there. Make it the new gossip place. Chuck the coffee or tea machine.

12. Cereal. Remember to only eat your handful. Pick a cereal without added sugar. Look at the ingredients.

13. Wholewheat toast with peanut butter, home made white butter, cheese, tofu spreads.

Notes

- Try to eat sitting crosslegged. You can do this even while sitting on a chair. If you can't, bring both legs up, and definitely try doing it even with one leg. (To send your blood to the stomach area.)
- Lunch is a good time to have a fatty acid supplement (flax seed, omega-3) as it improves insulin response.

- Don't have tea or coffee without eating anything (so, eat with your in between meal) and limit this to 2 a day.
- Offer 1 of these options to your clients or people you have to meet at work, instead of the regular chai and biscuits; you'll both end up eating healthier.
- If you have a lunch meeting, remember to eat a meal about 11 am from one of the options, and then at the restaurant, eat half of what you have on the plate. Then remember to eat your next meal after 2 hours.
- The more heavy options you can eat just before leaving from work. (You're dog-tired after a day's work and need the energy most then.)
- If you are going to workout immediately after work, have something from options 9 to 12 just as you set out.
- If it's going to be a stressful day, go for carb-rich options like cereal, poha, upma, etc.
- The basic principle of the in-between meals is to have low GI carbs with protein and fats. If you're being less active, you could just go for the protein and fat options like the peanuts, chana and cheese. (No food is really zero carb, and these will give you small amounts of carbs, protein and fat, stabilising blood sugar and giving you adequate energy.)

Step 5

Eat your dinner within 2 hours of sunset

Ideal: if the sun has set at 6 pm, eat dinner latest by 8 pm. Better still, have it by 7 pm. We already know that loading the stomach with dinner when it has little or no digestion capacity is a sure shot way to get fat (and to fame and recognition as the 'fat person in my building, office, college, school').

Let's get real: ok, so some of you are still in office, or travelling or waiting for others to get back home till 8 or 9 pm. Rethink 'dinner'. Have a healthy and nutritious meal between 6 to 7 pm; and then go for a token dinner later, ideally no later than 9 pm. You can have this first meal either before you leave from work, or in the car, or before you start preparing and planning for dinner if you are a homemaker. What this will ensure is that you are not ravenous by dinner time, or else you will overload your stomach when it can digest the least.

Some options for the early dinner or meal at 6 to 7 pm are (and there are a few other options above):

- Roti rolls: great for those who eat in transit. Roll what you fancy in the wholewheat roti: veggies, paneer, tofu, chicken, fish, omelette. You would probably need to bring these from home and refrigerate at work.
- Grilled sandwiches: ask for wholewheat bread, get the butter out, keep the cheese.

239

And always share this. The serving size in restaurants is always XL.

- Meal replacement powders which serve a minimum of 20 grams of protein, for the super duper no time to eat category. Mix in water or milk shake it. And then have it.
- Sprouts with dahi: more wholesome and easy to eat if you are having it before leaving from work or at home.
- Muesli with milk or curd or other whole grains like ragi, barley, mixed grains which you get in co-ops: especially if you are exhausted mentally, or a child, or an adult who goes to late evening workouts.
- Brown rice khichdi with paneer and veggies: keep the quantity right on this.
- A bowl of dal.
- Non-veg eaters, you can eat your chicken or fish at this time.

Notes

- If you are the type who needs 'comfort food' or reaches out for dessert when 'mentally fucked', or experiences road rage, you can't afford to ignore this step.
- You will discover more options on the way as you adopt this policy. But the principle of this meal is to go low on GI carbs and protein. My success with my clients rests on how well we plan this meal.

- Bad news. This meal is the biggest challenge. Good news: once you get this right, you are 99% on track.
- It is the best policy to adopt against overeating later. Don't skip this meal if you plan to drink later in the evening or are going out for a late evening dinner, entertaining clients, etc.
- If this is the time you are eating your early dinner and you aren't eating anything afterwards (ie, not doing the token dinner), remember only 2 things and nothing more. Your meal should be a combination of low GI carbs, fats and protein.

Token dinners

- Freshly cut veggies made into interesting salads (no dressing or sauces please)
- Dal with sabzi
- Stir fry with veggies of your choice
- Soups (but don't put them through a mixie)
- Grilled vegetables

Note

- Avoid carbs here, especially high GI ones like noodles, pasta, white rice, biscuits, pancakes, crepes, etc.

Step 6

Sleep at a fixed time

Ideally: sleep at the same time everyday. Always before midnight. In an ideal world, by 10.30 pm, after finishing off your last meal at 8 to 8.30 pm. Sleeping at the same time daily is the best gift that you can give yourself. It goes without saying that all those who sleep at a fixed time also wake up at the exact same time daily. Envy somebody's clear or ageless skin? Chances are your object of envy is sleeping at the exact same time daily. This is also one of the most safely and fiercely guarded secrets of some of the prettiest faces. A lot of women I have worked with in the film industry follow this rule. We think they are partying all night when in fact they are sleeping.

Let's get real: same time everyday? I sound like a Nazi don't I? How about giving yourself a 1 hour window? So you sleep daily between 10.30 to 11.30 pm. At least on the weekdays, and take the weekend off. But on all other days, guard your skin and keep your body young by keeping to your bedtime within the time limit.

10 things that will pull you back

1. Refusing to learn from experiences.
2. Believing that there is indeed a 'magical and quick' way to burn fat.

3. Not taking care of yourself. Depending on others to do this.
4. Being critical of yourself. Losing fat is about making progress, not about achieving perfection.
5. Eating too much at one time.
6. Eating after a long gap.
7. Taking a 'drink beer and laze around' holiday.
8. Expecting results in the first week.
9. 'Overdoing it and pushing yourself too far, to do whatever it takes.'
10. Not realising that there is much more to life than how much you weigh.

10 things that can take you forward on the path to staying fit

1. Cook something for yourself once every week. If you can't cook, learn to cook, even if its simple rice and dal. It will put you in touch with your kitchen and is an expression of love and compassion towards yourself. (Women, please cook a dish that is your favourite, not your spouse's, child's or neighbour's.)
2. Maintain silence as a regular practice. It could be a fixed hour or a few minutes every day, or an entire day once a month. If this is not possible, at least give up on 3 or 4 sentences (that you would normally not hold back).

But plan and stay with it. The tongue has to know that you are in control. (The tongue is also the main organ that controls what we eat, and we have to show our tongue who's the boss!)

3. Go without salt once every month. So eat according to the 4 principles, but just cut the salt from your diet. (Do this a day before that big party, for best results.)

4. Wake up just a little earlier than you are used to. And sleep just a little earlier too; 30 minutes is a good place to start.

5. Try and adopt the crosslegged posture while eating.

6. Also the squatting posture while shitting.

7. Keep up your favourite hobby, whatever it is; cricket, sitar, painting, acting, dancing or reading. Even an investment of as little as an hour a month makes life richer.

8. Take a Himalayan holiday and get off the touristy route—TREK. Great way to meet interesting people, and to be near untouched meadows, peaks and streams.

9. Learn something new every year. Keeps you young from within and it shows on the body. Being young is a state of mind where you feel free to be inquisitive and even stupid.

10. Get your family and friends to support you on your journey to getting fitter and leading a fulfilling life.

'Now' is the best time to start

The power of now. Hajaar books have been written on the power of now. Spiritual gurus ask us to stay in the now. Misery, fear, failure is in the past and future, in the now there is bliss (or so we are told).

So, stop waiting for the perfect time, when you will end the bad relationship, come out of a hectic work week, stop travelling, finish your exams, etc to start. Just start now. It is the perfect time to start. Let me tell you the story of a wise man and a fool. Both these men had a bowl and they had the task of collecting raindrops in the bowl. The wise man put his bowl out and collected a few drops every time it drizzled or rained a bit. The fool waited for the 'perfect time' when it would pour so that he could fill his bowl to the brim in no time. The wise man's bowl was full in no time, while the fool continued to wait for the perfect time.

So even if you can manage a little; a drop or a few drops, of the book right now, start collecting them *now* and in no time your bowl will be full with health, fitness and peace.

Fat is fit

My partner GP of 'Connect with Himalaya' was thrilled no end on hearing that Harish Kapadia (a walking talking encyclopaedia on the Indian Himalaya) would be visiting and staying the night on the same property where he and his group were camping. All day, he told the group stories and legends about Harish Kapadia. The number of books he has written, the mountains that he has climbed, the initiatives that he has started, etc. This obviously built a lot of expectation about India's most popular and loved mountain man. When he finally arrived, he was not exactly what the group imagined. He turned out to be an unassuming middle-aged man with a paunch.

'Aren't you little "healthy" for all the adventures you do,' asked one of the men from the group. Harish Kapadia was rather amused and declared that 'fat is fit'. (Now the buzz word of the group, albeit for all the wrong reasons.) And why not? It's stupid to measure fitness on the weighing scale or on a tape. If you can climb the biggest mountains in India, work for your community, write interesting books, narrate amazing stories, arrange seminars and talks on the Himalaya and their changing climates, and have a fan following amongst all age groups, then you are indeed fit. Fit to pursue your passion wholeheartedly and lead a fulfilling life. The point is to not just eat a wholesome diet, but also to lead a wholesome life!

Q&A

I want to know vitamin B12–rich sources in vegetarian options which I can get in day-to-day meals.
—Dr Arundhati Kulkarni, Poona

Vitamin B12 is one nutrient that we require in really tiny amounts. The daily recommended allowance for vitamin B12 is 1mcg (that's like 1/1000th of a gram) and even then its deficiency is widespread. There is no lack of vitamin B12 in the diet of a vegetarian—idli, dosa, ukkad, dhokla, lassi, dahi, nachni satva, usals or sprouts, even home-made pickles, are beautiful sources, low on cost, easy to procure and cook. More than the dearth of sources, it's the lifestyle that is making it difficult for the gut to absorb B12. Lack of exercise, low-fat diets, avoiding home-made ladoos (a rich source of minerals, fibre and essential fat) is making the digestion and assimilation of this micro-nutrient tougher. Throw in disturbed sleep or late nights, over-reliance on tea/coffee, consumption of biscuits regularly, social drinking and high stress levels and you have a system which is routinely low on B12 even after injections or megadoses of the vitamin. A complete lifestyle overhaul and learning to eat wholesome is what works like magic for B12.

And because B12 is also a cofactor in iron assimilation, it is critical that special attention is paid to this. Low iron levels come with their own issues of low energy levels, poor immunity and sugar cravings during PMS.

Do your celeb clients also follow the same rules like eating local food like rice?
—Reena Maldodi, Poona

Yes Reena, they are people too, just like you and me. And celeb or no celeb, the human physiology works the same way within each one of us. I guess each one of is seeking true love, good coffee and meaningful companionship.

So yes, they very much follow the same rules but, shall I say, with a different level of dedication altogether. I guess what makes people celebs is that they are ready to work harder than other people in their profession, that they are more committed, disciplined and passionate about what they do than your regular Joe, though most of us have a tough time seeing people from the glam world as more committed, disciplined, etc. And trust me, most actors have such a physically draining job that they are more than happy to come home to dal-chawal.

Can you please advise a diet chart for diabetics? What can be a replacement for rice as diabetics are not allowed to eat potatoes and rice? What should

be incorporated into their daily diet to keep blood sugar level in control?
—Jaspreet Saini, Mumbai

A diet chart for a diabetic wouldn't be too different from a non-diabetic. They would still need to follow the four basic principles and eat local, regional food, and stop before getting full. And then they would need to regularize their bedtimes and take to regular exercise. And no, rice is not the culprit here.

Rice, the way India eats it—with dal, dahi, kadhi, chana, rajma, legumes, milk, etc., and with ghee and some sabzi, actually turns into a low-glycemic-index meal. Buy local rice, try and get it hand-pounded or single-polished where it still looks more white than brown. Rice is in fact easy on the digestive system and I would recommend it to a diabetic. Happy to share that most of my clients who were on hypoglycemic drugs or insulin earlier are now off them, and rice is a daily part of their diet. Yes, they even eat it for dinner. It's about changing many things in one's lifestyle and not about switching from rice to chapati, biscuit to multigrain biscuit, sugar to sugar-free, etc. Also, how often do you eat potato really? If it's a part of aloo-gobhi that you eat once every week, please eat it. If you are eating french fries every day, then avoid it.

What type of purified water should we actually drink? Do today's purification processes actually deprive water of its natural minerals and vitamins? Is the age-old method of just boiling water enough

to kill all bacteria and make the water safe for drinking?
—Shobhana Rakesh, Chennai

Water is as essential as oxygen for every living being on earth. I mean the main reason why we feel that there is life on Mars is because they have found water on Mars. Traditional purification—boiling, filtering and storing in earthen matkas—is the only real purification where you don't take anything away from the water, it retains everything that makes the water unique—its flavour, colour and aroma. The commercial purification process not just robs water of minerals and of its uniqueness, but the fact that it stores water in plastic containers which can never be washed or accessed robs water of its purity. Safe drinking water is what is used locally and ethically. The so-called safe packaged water uses groundwater that actually belongs to communities which live in that area, also called as ecological wealth, which shouldn't really be anyone's property. Moreover it takes anywhere from 2 to 7 litres of water to 'produce' 1 litre of water and then there is the cost of the plastic that we will leave behind for generations together as landfills. Overall I feel that, for our country, where women walk miles for water, we are better off sticking to our traditional methods. Get it checked in any lab and you will find that it really is purer and safer than we would like to give it credit.

Because of work, I am constantly on the move. My projects are in different cities (75 minutes flying time one way), so I spend a lot of time in taxis, traffic and flights. What would be best meal option to cope with the additional stress/ requirement? Also what meal options should I carry for lunch/dinner if I would like to avoid outside/hotel food during the 2–3 days travel?
—Anjali Kiran, Sweden

Wow, Anjali! Sounds super hectic, you sure must love your job to keep up with that kind of schedule. Here are some of my favourite options—cheese, dates, nuts, home made ladoos (will be great for you to pick up on a home-made ladoo recipe from a family elder, it's like genetic medicine. If you were US-, UK-, SA- or Australia-based, I would have said 'look for an aunty' because there is always someone offering fresh home-made Indian delicacies). At the airport you can always buy fruit yogurt and fresh fruit (whole, not cut) to eat later during the drive or in between meetings. Cashews are great for keeping travel-related bloating down because of their iron, fibre and vitamin B content. For lunch and dinner options—thepla with chutney or dahi, peanut butter or cheese or avocado sandwich are good options. Another thing is to roast dal and rice till it's totally dry and add salt, spices, and then cook it in the microwave on site or in the hotel. If a microwave is not available, complain to the HR.

The new fad is cold-pressed juices. I have tried them. They are very tasty but are they healthy too? If they are, what combo should they be had in and at what time of the day?
—Malav Mehta, Mumbai

Basically any box that you can open for detox, cleansing, fat burn, etc., is a wonderful revenue model and gets the cash registers ringing. It takes more than a beautiful revenue model to give you detox, cleanse, fat loss though. You need to open your heart and think, how fresh is the kale/apple in my 'fresh juice'? I recently tweeted that all of us who are gifted with gums and teeth can just make the cold-pressed juice in our own mouth. That's when it really works wonders. Eating a whole fruit would also mean that you take the pains to actually visit the market and pick the fresh fruit or seasonal vegetable yourself—that way even the main ingredient's purity, freshness, wholesomeness are guaranteed. So yes, maintaining good health requires investment of more than just money.

The other factor to consider is that there are lots of studies linking fructose (fruit sugar) to metabolic diseases—right from obesity to heart diseases and everything in between. Typically, if you eat a fruit, it takes longer than drinking a juice, it would not just give you more satiety but also the quantity of the fruit consumed is smaller than when it is drunk as juice. Also, nutrient delivery to the cells is altered the minute you juice something outside instead of inside the mouth. I suspect it changes the way the body deals with the fructose then, especially given the fact that it will come in higher quantities and faster speed compared to when eaten.

It is also about how you sell an idea. The good old aamras never got sold to us as cold-pressed, handcrafted, polyphenols and fibre-enriched juice so we treat it with suspicion and link it to obesity. Not fair! We had it purely for its heavenly taste, and that's the foolproof way to eat a fruit.

How true are the claims made by vegans about the malpractices in the dairy industry and the benefits/harmful effects of milk?
—Anupama S. Joshi, Mumbai

Quite true, I am afraid. Someone on my Facebook page just recommended that we need to have a 'KYM—Know Your Milkman' process in place to ensure that we are not just buying good-quality but also ethically produced milk. Milk has unfortunately swung from one end of the pendulum to another. So medical schools with their limited nutrition syllabi would qualify milk as an anti-carcinogenic, and once in practice, when the doctor attends a CME (Continuing Medical Education), she would learn that it actually causes cancer.

The trouble is not really the milk but the source that it is coming from, the method of procurement and finally the way it is treated once it's in the factory. Indians, in fact Asians and Africans, have celebrated milk and milk products—dahi, chaas, makhan, ghee—for its therapeutic value for centuries now. It is sourced from the native indigenous varieties of cows; after the calf has had its share, it is sold fresh and as whole milk without being treated (exposed to sudden and extreme hot and low temperatures) in factories. The desi cow milk is naturally rich in vitamin D, the hump which is unique to the indigenous breeds does the job of adding vitamin D to the milk. Also, this milk is rich in A2 type of protein (as against the A1 protein in commercial milk), which is known to reduce the risk of diabetes. Desi cow milk is therefore highly recommended, and if you can't find a desi cow, go for buffalo milk.

The USA has something called as the Bramhan Breeders Association where native Indian cows are cross-mated with the local variety so that the new breed is sturdier and the milk richer in nutrients and pleasing in flavour. Anyway, the trend of grass-fed versus corn-fed, free-grazing versus chained, cow milk is now a popular peg for selling ethical milk. In the West, you can even buy what is called 'raw milk', the kind of milk which retains the good bacteria, vitamins and minerals. It is exactly the same milk that your milkman brings home every morning but then in the food industry what goes out of fashion in one continent is considered most fashionable in another. Or like Archana Puran Singh would say, what's LS in one part of the world is HS or exotic in another.

I'm an image consultant and a tarot-card reader. I lost approximately 12 kg after reading and following your book. Big thanks to you. My problem is that I am so used to eating every 2–3 hours that I'm incapable of fasting now. Whenever I read about the benefits of fasting, I feel so helpless. Is fasting really beneficial for immunity-building? If yes how do I redevelop fasting skills?
—Anu Mittal, New Delhi

That is just so amazing, Anu! Congrats and thanks for sharing your journey. The thing with fasting is that you learn to keep a little space empty in your stomach and not fill it to the brim. If you are eating every 2–3 hours, you are already doing that. As for the immunity, cleansing and other fasting benefits, one must remember that upavas is a spiritual practice, where eating restriction is only one of the disciplines to be followed.

You can fast for a change because from kuttu to samo-chawal, coconut water to groundnuts, fruits to dry fruits, all the yummy stuff is allowed on a fast. You can eat these once every 2–3 hours. Eating fried, packaged banana or potato chips is neither a fast nor discipline, nor is starving and causing harm to the body recommended as a spiritual practice. So like the Buddha said, walk the Madhyama marga, the golden median.

Just like 'murgi pehle ya anda' I want to ask u 'hypothyroidism pehle ya weight gain'? As it is

universally known that low metabolism causes storage of fat around the body, a person with hypothyroidism needs to keep activities high in order to maintain weight. But it wasn't known that bad eating habits cause hypothyroidism.
—Sonal Modak, Belapur

Who came first depends on what time zone you are currently looking at. Lifestyle is very much a contributing factor to every metabolic disease including hypothyroidism. Poor eating habits, lack of exercise, sedentary job and stress are just some of the critical lifestyle factors that affect the thyroid metabolism. So a poor lifestyle may create an issue with the thyroid and a disciplined lifestyle may avoid the expression of a thyroid disorder even when there is a genetic history.

The ball thankfully is in our court. Irrespective of the cause, the thyroid likes to be in a body that eats fresh and in regulated quantities, sleeps and wakes up at the same time every day, exercises as regularly as bathing, etc. My clients who strength-train and practise classical yoga not only lose weight but are even able to bring the dosages of their medicine down if not completely get off it.

Patronise a doctor who tells you to correct your lifestyle and promotes exercise versus the one who tells you to 'lose 5 kilos' to help your thyroid. That's because even starvation or calorie restriction and walking may help you lose a little weight initially but it surely doesn't help the thyroid gland feel any better nor does it help you lower your meds. Whatever comes or goes first, lifestyle correction works and is critical to good thyroid metabolism.

A question that has been nagging me is why most nutritionists and dietitians do not know their facts right. Why do they mislead people? After all, they must have studied the same curriculum as you did. Then why is there so much misinformation floating around owing to what dietitians tell us. For example, a friend of mine was asked by her dietitian to have only veg sandwiches for dinner for one whole week. Obviously, my friend could not stick to this plan for more than 4 days but still she was all praises for her.
—Vipasha Adlakha, Navi Mumbai

Someone once said that education ruined us. I guess that's the case with at least nutrition education in our country. The curriculum in nutrition colleges is exactly what it is in rest of the institutions across India—not updated or regionalized or even Indianised for that matter. But then globally there is a huge challenge of coming out with nutrition advice that is real, doable and practical.

Also what I studied as part of my PG in sports science and nutrition is mostly counting calories, making food exchange charts (where a pizza slice of 100 cal is of the same worth as dahi chawal of 100 cal) and cooking meals with as little oil as possible. My internship involved planning diets for athletes in Sports Authority of India, Gandhinagar campus, providing them with 'nourishment' in less than Rs 36 per athlete per day. At a week-long internship at the Army Sports Institute, Pune, a major who was teaching sports physiology to my batch of 7 girls (nutrition colleges only have girl students, for some reason) was so disgusted with our poor knowledge and crappy attitude that he refused to teach us for the rest of the week. He said that thr entire country should be ashamed that there is a species called dietitians who wore white coats and earned more money for not valuing the nation's dharohar of food wisdom than a jawan who would toil hard to preserve every stone of the country.

Anyway, emotional speeches aside, the problem lies in the way we learn nutrition right from school. Orange is taught as a source of vitamin C in the land of amlas, carrot is a source of vitamin A and not ghee, protein comes from only dal, pulses, milk and meat and not from rajgeera chiki or panjiri. So the same thing carries on even when one 'specializes' in nutrition education, there is no understanding or value of traditional food wisdom. Anyway a 3- or even a 30-year degree cannot be an alternative to the rich food wisdom that is easily accessible in our homes. For a country where education is transmitted and refined in guru–shishsya parampara, nutrition colleges should only teach us to back our traditional wisdom with nutrition jargon and encourage diversity within cultures. Instead we are going towards everyone eating a uniform diet—cereal and milk in the morning, sandwich for lunch, grilled chicken breast for dinner.

Food and nutrition is a subject that is all encompassing and cannot be studied properly even in a lifetime. That's one of the reasons why I update myself with at least one course every year in the Himalaya, studying the Indian philosophy of food and well-being, and one in the West studying what the high-tech labs are saying about the same subject. Over the last decade I have seen the same trend—the labs catching up with grandma's age-old wisdom and validating everything she said and showing what we discarded as superstition as scientific.

The reason why standardized guidelines—avoid calories, fat, carbs, drink juices, eat fibre biscuits, etc.—work is because everyone, from the doctor to the dietitian to the trainer, says the exact same thing. It's the power of consistent information, however misleading. It's like what the medics say about statins: You wake up a cardiologist in the middle of the night and ask, 'Statins are . . .?' and he will reply, 'Life-saving.' It is consistent information for years together. Doesn't matter, the endless data complied on their use, abuse and side effects. No doctor will ever say exercise is life-saving and therefore our ability to stick or comply to exercise is so much poorer if not entirely non-existent as compared to popping a statin.

I can also understand your friend's praise for her dietitian; we don't value diet advice for being real and practical but for its ability to challenge us. Can I starve, do I have the willpower and do I have what it takes to be thin? We have been systematically cultivated by the weight loss industry to use methods, however harmful, for 'results', however short-lived. So what can I say, it takes courage to eat right, it takes even more courage to know that your body doesn't change overnight. And that too for a culture whose foundation is 'vasudaiva kutumbakam', it takes faith and trust in our oral heritage to eat in a manner that is sustainable for both the earth and the human being.

These days obesity in children is a major concern. How does one educate and encourage them from the beginning to love healthy eating and a healthy lifestyle so that it doesn't become an ordeal for the entire family later on?
—Vanita Gupta, Jalandhar

Kya bolu, Vanita, it's just scary, this whole childhood obesity thing. Kids seem to move less today than even 7–8 years earlier. There was an outrage when Barbie was gifted as a toy but it is not unusual today to see even 2-year-olds own mini iPads; poor Barbie pales in comparison. The startling factor though is that there is no outrage, almost a silent acceptance that children MUST have some gadget—if not an iPad, a smartphone—to entertain themselves and to stay connected.

First things first—if we want them to eat right, we must teach them to pay attention. Only when you pay attention to what you eat can you tell what to eat and what to leave on your plate. For that, as parents, we must curtail use of gadgets ourselves, not watch TV or read newspapers during meal times and adopt a more active lifestyle.

Children need at least 90 minutes of activity every single day and as parents that's the first thing we must look to provide. More importantly they must play in an unstructured fashion which allows them to learn a lot of life skills—be it negotiation or simply the importance of fair play. Along with that, if we can encourage them to take up a sport actively, it will be great. But what we must remember is that they have to learn that staying active or exercising is a non-negotiable aspect of life, the only way they can learn that is if we as parents are making time to work out regularly.

For kids to value local food, we must value and practice the art of using local produce, and cook using regional, traditional recipes. Our children must be educated about our diverse food culture and their taste for our traditional and nutritious food must be cultivated with care and patience. With this they must be taught to deconstruct media messages—things like 'are you really a samajhdar mummy if you buy a certain brand of cornflakes' or 'can you really run fast by eating biscuits' or 'are instant noodles really a quick, nutritious meal'. Basically, if we understand that good health doesn't come from packaged food, even if these packets come with iron shakti or plastic toys. Education, including food education, is what will empower our children to make the right choices today and for the rest of their lives.

Above all, parents must learn to guide kids, helping them understand that playing games on PlayStation or Xbox doesn't qualify as playing, watching videos on phones is not entertainment and speaking to classmates over chat groups is not friendship. We need a multi-pronged approach where everyone involved in a child's welfare—parents, schools and even the government—takes active part. The recent Equal Streets initiative in Mumbai is one such example.

What diet do you recommend for people with high uric acid, vitamin D deficiency and arthritis? Eating more eggs and chana causes pain in joints.
—Sonia Sakhuja, Yamuna Nagar

One of the main reasons that vitamin D deficiency is spreading like an epidemic is that dietary fat has almost disappeared from our diets. Not because it doesn't exist but because we have gone out of our way to eat low-fat or zero-fat everything—milk to dahi to even ice creams. Ghee is something that we look at like a villain, and then, of course, we move very little, mostly leading really sedentary lives. Now, vitamins A, E, D and K are all fat-soluble, which means that in the absence of dietary fat, no amount of sunbathing, injections or megadoses of vitamin D will help you assimilate vitamin D.

In 2013, Sweden was the first developed country to say that its dietary guidelines of reducing fat intake were wrong. The US FDA has done the same now. Ayurveda, on the other hand, has for thousands of years guided us to eat wholesome meals based on the season and not based on carbs, proteins and fats. The traditional way of life has also been to include ghee in every meal we eat, which is a great way to avoid vitamin D deficiency. Even better if we use desi cow milk to make dahi, makhan and ghee as it is naturally rich in vitamin D and the vitamin can be absorbed better than when it is added artificially to milk. And no, naturally existing saturated fat in the diet, i.e. milk and milk products, nuts, egg yolk, and even sensible use of meat is not a threat to either uric acid or heart diseases.

For uric acid, it's important to avoid alcohol, long gaps in meals and sugar-loaded goodies like muffins, biscuits, chocolates, etc. Unfortunately, the popular advice is always to avoid dals and certain vegetables and not the list above. So avoid what really exposes you to high uric acid levels, take to regular exercise, regularize your bedtime and feel free to eat your dal with your rice/chapati and your occasional meats too.

As south Indians, our staple diet is rice. These days everyone is against eating rice. I am confused. Are wheat, jowar, ragi and bajra better than rice?
—Rohini R. Rao, Bangalore

That's like asking if eating paratha is better than eating idli. It is best to stick to what has proved itself to be genetically compliant and suits the region and the climatic conditions that come with it. Rice is as ancient as Indian civilization and thayir sadam, dahi bhat, kadhi chawal or Hyderabadi biryani, the various preparations that we make out of our rice, are odes to India's sophisticated and evolved culinary heritage.

In my opinion, we should be grateful for the many recipes that have been handed down to us, where we have learnt to make everything from a really light to a really celebratory meal out of rice—from kanji to bisibille and everything in between.

Rice is a complete meal by itself, a good source of amino acids, specially the branched chain amino acids, which are linked to increasing fat metabolism and to giving the mind a sense of calm. Little wonder then that most of us are eager to come back home to a meal of hot rice and dal. Rice is also negligible if not completely zero on fat. And no, it is not high in starch, unless of course you are eating uncooked, raw rice.

As for glycemic index, India has more than 1000 varieties of rice and all of them are medium in GI, which means that they lead to a slow, steady rise in the blood sugar. Eat the rice that is local to your region, eat hand-pounded or single-polished white rice, cook rice the way that blends the best with the other preparations that you make and not according to what is 'highest' in fibre. Also know that eating rice with dahi, ghee, milk, pulses, veggies, the way Indians consume rice, makes it safe for diabetics and overweight people to consume it. So please go ahead and eat it, rice is nice.

As for jowar, bajra, nachni, eat them too. They are precious; the West is calling them 'ancient' grains. And eat them the way they should be eaten, for their own sake, for their unique taste, not as a replacement for rice. Bangalore also has a culture of eating ragi balls with chutney, right?

I have read a lot about gluten on the Internet, and now I am confused about consuming it. We have grown up eating poli (chapati), and wheat, which mainly consist of gluten. What is the use of gluten to our body?
—Rasika Joshi, Singapore

Gluten is simply a general name for protein found in grains like wheat, rye, barley, etc. It is responsible for nourishing the plant embryo and later giving shape to the dough of the flour. That's exactly why you can give atta any shape you like—chapati, phulka, rotla, bhati; it is even turned into a diya during festivals.

What I find amazing is that on the one hand the weight-loss industry urges us to consume more protein and on the other hand discriminates against poor gluten. While celiac disease is a real issue, most gluten avoiders belong to the category which is trying this as another way to lose weight. Sab try kar liya, abhi yeh bhi type. Amazingly, most gluten avoiders also feel 'better' and this is called as the classic 'nocebo' effect. A cousin of placebo, nocebo means that you believe that something is working for you even while it may be harming you.

From the Last Supper to the Bhatinda ka dhaba, everyone has broken bread in their own unique way and it has sustained civilizations. Imagine Italian men, their fabled sex appeal and now take out the pasta. If you changed what they ate, they wouldn't look as good or speak as charmingly. Anyway, this nocebo has spun off an entire industry of gluten-free products that is worth at least 10 billion dollars. That's a lot of money—enough to keep convincing wheat-eaters that somehow the magic lies in avoiding it.

Not just muffins and bread, you even have gluten-free dating sites now. There you go, it's in your face, and it's going to go the 'avoid fat' way. A few years later, there will be enough studies proving beyond reasonable doubt that avoiding gluten has led to multiple other issues and nutritional deficiencies. There is a growing recognition of what is called as 'non-nutrient compounds' within food. So when you avoid wheat, you are not just avoiding gluten but many known and unknown nutrients that are responsible in nourishing your tissues. So really, if you have been eating chapatis, pooris and atte ka sheera aka prasad at gurudwaras, and found yourself asking for second helpings, know that the way we eat wheat is a sensible way of consuming it— as a part of a wholesome meal. And that just because gluten-free products are at least 40% more expensive than gluten-wala products, they are not necessarily good for you; they are only good for the weight-loss market making money out of the latest monster.

I agree that we should eat whatever our ancestors ate. My questions is, should we really eat grains? What about Paleo diet which our ancestors used to eat around 10,000 years back before humans started agriculture? Researcher says that human genes are still the same as they were 10,000 years back. It did not change. (Paleo diet consists of vegetables, fruits, game meat or organically grown meat, and nuts. No dairy, no grains.) What is your take on this?
—Shilpa Pate Dashpute, Los Angeles

Yes, you are right. Our genes haven't changed, but the way they interact with the environment has changed because the environment has changed drastically.

Food not only makes our bodies, it also makes our mind. The subtle life-force prana, the intelligence, etc. is what our ancient sciences and culture teach us. In the Himalayan valley called Vyas (after the Vyas muni), there is a tradition of eating kuttu ka atta. All of Vyas's power—be it sexual or his sharp intellect or his ability to dictate the Mahabharata—comes from it. But mythology aside, India, China and the most ancient, and therefore the more evolved civilizations, have grown and celebrated rice (Mohenjo-daro had a flourishing trade in grains.) Both India and China offer rice even to the dead; so if you are born into this DNA and gene pool, I doubt you can escape it.

The game changer in any diet is what the latest villain gets replaced with. When fat was the villain in the 70s, it got replaced with sugar, and low-fat products flooded the market. Today sugar or carb is the villain and fat is gaining newfound glory. Soon the villain is going to be protein, veganism is one of the proofs of that. Time and again, at least modern nutrition history teaches us that when you make a villain out of a food product, 30 years later it comes back as the hero, and what replaced it becomes the new villain. Learning from history is crucial, especially for fitness professionals. You don't want to be 'out of fashion' 30 years later. Making a villain out of any food group, invariably leads to health issues, the carb-fever in the case of Paleo, where the body suffers from mild fever to full-blown adrenal fatigue and hormonal imbalance.

As for Paleo, it allows nuts, which are just like grains—cultivated, not exactly growing in the wild.

The 'game' meat is not hunted with boulders and arrows but bought from a counter. So the risk of the genes interacting with the new environment is still very much prevalent. And what about the grain-free muffins and protein-rich cookies? Did the hunter–gatherer breed also make time to bake while living in their caves? For a culture like ours, which doesn't open boxes for breakfast or goes 'take out' for lunch/dinner, the meat-based diet is more refined and not 'wilder' or coarser than what we are currently eating.

So I guess one needs to give one's ancestors more credit than being hunters and gatherers and not overlook the value of eating wholesome, local and home-cooked food irrespective of where one lives. Let's acknowledge that ours is the culture of yoga and Ayurveda, with a legacy of food wisdom that made human life more meaningful and joyful and didn't reduce the goal of human existence to weight loss and a six pack.

Oil is an essential ingredient in Indian cooking and most other cuisines as well. Could you please list out the healthier ones and demystify the hype (or is it myth?) around olive oil? Also, which oil is the best for fried food and can it be reused?
—Sangeetha Rajankar, Chennai

Virgin olive oil is marketed in India with great fanfare; it gets displayed at expos where European cuisine is projected as better, cooler and with an in-your-face attitude of the good-for-us desi public. Celeb chefs, skinny hostesses and hard-to-miss displays at kiosks are only part of the strategy. In my kind of business it is routine to get promotional emails about virgin olive oil all the time.

A year ago I was invited to Jordan to speak about yogic wisdom about food to a group of business heads and I asked them what they thought of the fuss about olive oil. 'Another laugh of the West,' said a sharp-looking businessman to me. 'We eat olives all the time, in chutney or ripe, in salads or pickle, as oil or paste and then the West says it's good for the heart, blah blah. Isn't laughing good for the heart, ha? But it's free, so no use.'

It's great to have olive oil while you are trekking in Petra or boating in Venice, if you are an Italian or a Jordanian. But when you are home, please use local oils that don't just blend well but also enhance the flavour of local ingredients and recipes. So either filtered groundnut oil or mustard oil or coconut oil, based on the region you come from. Even sesame oil that is used over malgapudi, or gun powder as it is called in Mumbai, is great with idlis.

Each one of these local oils can be used for all cooking purposes—from tadka to stir-frying to deep-frying. However none of them should be reused for deep-frying, the only cooking medium which deserves that honour is desi ghee and that's thanks to its high smoking point. So ghee, or nei as it's known in Chennai, is an undervalued champion and it is currently on the high streets of NYC for its fat-burning and anti-ageing properties. It has a new name there—clarified butter.

Now I wish the Indian government, dieticians, doctors and celeb chefs championed the cause of local oils and ghee, like the EU does for olive oil, but then, as they say, truth will always find a way to show up no matter how much you hide it. So I guess we must sing the glories of our oils and the therapeutic ghee before the West or the weight-loss industry does.

I am an obstetrician working in my own maternity home at Sangamner near Nasik. I followed your advice strictly, started eating 8 meals a day, joined the gym, and achieved great results—10 kg weight loss and increased vigour in my day-to-day activity. As an obstetrician I have to attend emergency calls at night. If I have to wake up at 2 a.m., should I eat anything before going back to sleep?
—Amit Shinde, Nasik

That's amazing! Congrats, Doctor sahib! I feel particularly happy when doctors, CAs, lawyers, the padha–leekha variety, exercise, because then it becomes an aspirational thing for us, the rest of the junta, to do.

Waking up in the middle of the night is an occupational hazard for you and the best way to ensure that you are nutritionally equipped to deal with it for the rest of your life is to have a food/ eating strategy. These are your options:

1. If you have worked out that day, then have some dry fruits when you wake up at 2 a.m.

2. If you haven't worked out, then you can go attend the emergency provided you have had the time to eat a wholesome dinner; if not, use option 1.

3. Before going to bed, having cashews or gulkand soaked in milk is a good option. They will help recover from disturbed sleep and have a calming effect on both the mind and the stomach.

All the best and keep progressing on your fitness journey!

For others who may not even have the option of sleeping a few hours in the night because of shift duties that start late in the evening and end early in the morning, here are the options:

1. Start your day with a fresh fruit, preferably a banana—good on the stomach, available year-round and the best way to beat dehydration that sets in because of AC offices, laptop radiation and late nights.
2. Breakfast should be wholesome; some of the options are poha, upma, idli, dosa, paratha, dalia, roti-chutney, eggs and toast.

3. Follow the four principles, eat every 2 hours and some of the options are peanuts, fruit, chaas, lassi, cheese, chiki, home-made ladoos.

4. Main meal options are roti-sabzi-dahi, rice-dal-sabzi, pulao-raita, khichdi-dahi, etc. Keep it simple and eat home-cooked food. It may sound too simplistic but it's really the best way to look your age, otherwise night shifts always make people look older than they are.

5. Workout 150 minutes a week, that's like thrice a week, and plan your days in advance. Get at least one session of weight training and the best time is 60–90 minutes post breakfast as by that time your body would have recovered from working till late.

6. Even though food is free in office, stay off junk that comes out of the packaged products including chips, sodas and juices.

7. Stay hydrated.

All the best and hope this helps.

How do we know if we are really fit for our age? Losing weight and inches is one thing, but how does one determine fitness levels with age? What are the clinical attributes that we should be aware of?
—Anisha Mohanty, Gurgaon

For starters, just as we like to earn more money with age, we should earn more fitness with age. And that's really easy—all it takes is an investment of 150 minutes per week in exercise that challenges the body's current strength, flexibility and stamina. I have written about this in detail in my third book, *Don't Lose Out, Work Out!*

Age doesn't make us old or unfit, but inactivity coupled with poor eating habits and undisciplined lifestyle sure does. Just some of the parameters of knowing that you are fit for your age are:

1. You wake up with enthusiasm, not needing an alarm and surely not putting the alarm on snooze.
2. You sleep soundly and don't need any pills to go to bed.
3. You exercise as a way of life and not as a boring chore you have to do.
4. Running up or down the stairs is no big deal for you.
5. You trek at least once every year.
6. You don't need a porter to pick luggage off the belt at an airport, let alone needing a wheelchair when you travel abroad.
7. You never need to stand on a weighing scale because you always feel light on your feet and in your body.
8. And above all you understand that fitness is not some statistical or mathematical measurement but an experience of freedom and joy within the body.

You always stress on the principle of 'Think global, eat local'. How does this apply to Indians living abroad? What is local for them—the food they grew up on or the local food at the location?
—Akanksha Minocha Sharma, Munich

Thanks for the question, Akanksha. Not just living abroad but even living within India is such a diverse experience. The food and eating habits of, say, Chennai is alien to Delhi, other than idli, dosa, which is pan-Indian. But the dosa of Delhi can't be eaten by a person from Chennai. Then of course, most of the food from the North-east, even Darjeeling, can't even be pronounced by people from Kolkata. So let me say what Nehru said—Unity in diversity.

A subhashit in Sanskrit says that every person has a different temperament, every pond has different water, every community has a different conduct or code of ethics and every mouth speaks a different language. Nothing would describe India better and then when people from this diverse country go abroad there are even more influences from the karma bhoomi. Well, what works in our favour is that we are adaptable and can quickly blend influences into our routine life.

The easiest thing to do is to keep all dry ingredients like rice, wheat, grains, dals, pulses, ghee, jaggery, etc., Indian, and fruits and veggies local to the place you are living. For UK, the closest tomatoes are from Spain and bhendi is from Kenya. So make the ladoos, chiki, paratha, halwas and rice the way you learnt to make it, and for vegetables and salads use the stuff you use from the farmers' market.

Similarly, when you are in India but have parents from different cultures or grew up in a small village in Punjab but now work in Pune/Gurgoan/Bangalore, just make the best of both the worlds and contribute and learn to cook at least one regional dish of every parent or your partner in your kitchen without posting it on Instagram. Just keep it real, okay?

'Visceral Fat'—how does one reduce this adamant and resilient matter? I follow your guidelines religiously, and exercise following principles of your phenomenal work *Don't Lose Out, Work Out!* Changes physically and mentally are abundant, no doubt. But this internal-fat burning is so slow, sometimes demotivating, to even tougher guys. Any further advice from the toughest adversary of Fat India is eagerly awaited.
— Shashi Dhara, Bangalore

Shashi sir, move. Sitting is the new smoking as you have read on the cover of *Don't Lose Out, Work Out!* And before more gyan, congrats on following the principles of exercising right and experiencing the changes within, always feels so good to hear that.

Two things you can do to accelerate fat metabolism: include ghee in every meal and coconut at least once a day, even as a garnish on vegetables and dal. The unique fatty acid molecules in these two foods make it easier for our body to specifically mobilize fatty acids from stubborn fat areas.

In terms of activity, know that if you work out but are inactive during the day, then the results you get from the workout are limited, slow and compromised. In terms of actual exercise, optimize time spent on strength training that utilizes the big muscle groups—legs, back and chest.

More importantly, are you eating the post-workout meal and following the 4 Rs of post-workout meal for good recovery? And know that the most undervalued aspect of losing fat is good restorative sleep. Read the sleep strategies from *Women and the Weight Loss Tamasha* (because it applies equally to both genders) and ensure that you are not compromising on that. Compromised sleep always leads to slower recovery and therefore results.

Above all, be patient, kind and good to your body. It takes years and years for us to collect body fat, give it some time to lose it too. A thumb rule is that, if it took you 10 years to get fat, invest at least 10 months of consistent exercise, eating right and disciplined bedtimes before losing patience with your body or breaking your own heart.

Exercise is like investing in the share market, if you have taken a disciplined and scientific approach then it may test your patience but will reward your conviction.

We see a lot of 'health experts' claiming sugar to be evil. However, I believe that sugar is essential for one's well-being. Should one completely quit using sugar? Also, if white/refined sugar is bad then what are the better options and how much sugar must one consume daily?
—Sumit Kain, New Delhi

Yes, you are right, the misinformation around sugar runs so deep that it's also a sad tale of how this ancient nutrient (yep, I wrote nutrient) is now just looked down upon. We just 'know' that it's harmful for 'normal' people and a killer for 'diabetics'.

Here's the truth: Sugar has been celebrated as a panch amrit in our culture along with milk, honey, ghee and curd. The weight-loss industry has brainwashed us to look down upon each of them and it is the reputation of sugar that has taken the maximum beating. Sugar is not the white killer. In fact, ancient Egypt used it as a healer on wounds, way before antibiotics came into existence.

What's harmful is the way we are using sugar now—in biscuits, pastries, cakes, chocolates, etc., where, other than the fact that massive amounts of sugar is used, there is an overload of preservatives, trans fats, salts, emulsifiers and lack of essential fibre and minerals. Of course, we choose to overlook this fact and instead attach all harmful effects of these to sugar. Then, all the weight-loss industry does is to create another market for 'diet' foods. The preservatives, trans fats and emulsifiers stay, and sugar gets replaced with a sweetener. And we are told that this mixture will make us thin and prevent diabetes and heart disease. Really?

So put that spoon of sugar into your tea or coffee; even if calories haunt you, it's only 20 calories; you probably burnt that much by just reading this answer. One gulab jamun or peda won't kill you either. What will harm you is that nutrient-bereft pizza, burger, juices, cookie or cake that you ate unthinkingly. And that sweetener you virtuously put in your tea.

Appendix

1   Kareena ka *Tashan*

'Hello? Why is your cell switched off? Bebo's been trying to get in touch with you ya.'

'My battery went off,' I managed.

'Get a new phone now,' said Shaira, as she hung up. Kareena was one of her closest friends. Shaira had been on the diet plan for a while, had dropped her body fat levels, and was now looking gorgeous within 2 months of delivering her second baby.

Even while we spoke there was beep after beep; messages on my now active cell phone.

I started reading one message after another. 'Thanks for being there luv, lost 4 kilos'; 'Hey guess what, I am fitting in my 1986 jeans, saved it from college time. Muah'; 'Can you give me an option, I will puke if I see muesli now'; 'Maam, I am sick. wont come to the gym today'; etc etc... till I came across this one:

'Hi, this is Kareena Kapoor. I hv bn trying to get in touch with you but your cell is swtchd off. I have heard so much about you. Got your no frm Shaira. Wats a gud time to call? Thanks.'

'What?' I thought to myself. Read it again. And then I got back to answering all the smses on the phone and pushed Kareena Kapoor's message out of my mind—it was clearly a bad joke. How could she be so normal and real? No middle men calling? Nobody calling to say 'Tumhari to life ban gayee. Madam/sir milna chahte hain.'

I had nearly made up my mind not to call, but then reminded myself that when I first heard from Anil Ambani, it had happened in a very 'normal' way too.

'Hello Rujuta, Mr Anil Ambani would like to speak to you. When would you be free to talk?' The real stars never display any 'starry' behaviour I guess.

So I called back on Kareena's number. 'Yeh mera dil pyaar ka deewana,' went the ring tone. The tension built. At the time, everybody was talking about how hot and 'healthy' she looked in the song with SRK (its one of the remixes, I love).

'HI!!! How are you... I have been trying to call you ALL of yesterday... '

We decided to meet the day after.

Shaira had warned me that Kareena is 'Too down to earth and simple ya,' but I still didn't know what to expect. When I met Kareena, she was wearing tracks and a ganji with hair piled up in a ponytail.

'HI!! [I later came to realise this is her trademark high energy greeting] F-i-n-a-l-l-y! How much I tried to call you... Shaira is looking so good ya.'

A glowing complexion (Kapoor trademark), sans make up (even moisturiser), sparkling, intelligent eyes, an animated and almost childlike expression; unassuming, head on her shoulders, feet on the ground. This was the enigma called Kareena Kapoor.

'Hey, you look really good in *Don* and even better in person,' I told her.

'Thanks,' said Kareena and smiled genuinely. I knew her critics and rivals had made rude comments about how she looked in the gold coloured dress which she had worn in that number, so I was quite taken aback by her plain and simple thanks. Not once did she say anything like, 'Yeah, but I need to lose weight.' No pointing or pinching of body parts and saying, 'Yeh jaana chaiye.'

The most striking aspect of Bebo's personality is that she shows unconditional love and acceptance towards her body. She is not the type to hold herself at ransom on the weighing scale. 'Listen, I just get so confused with what to eat ya, especially when I am shooting out of Mumbai. Sometimes my system feels very disturbed, at times I am bloated. I workout very regularly, hardcore. From struggling to do 5 to 6 suryanamaskars, I am doing 50 aaram se now. My strength and stamina is good. Now I want to get all lean and toned.'

Like most of us, Bebo was confused. Fat-free or low carb, almost everybody, on the set, shoots and parties, had an opinion on what was the best diet, and which would yield maximum results. The 'expert' opinions didn't help either. Dieting, as I have said before, is synonymous to starving or eating yucky food, and this was not something she could ever bring herself to do. People around her were on juices, soups and salad, etc in the name of diets and these things didn't appeal to her. 'I think all this is a perversion,' she told me.

'You know, I have to wear a bikini for this new movie I am doing, *Tashan*. I want to feel comfortable wearing it, for that I need to get all lean.' 'When I saw Shaira eating all the time, kabhi peanuts, cheese, roti, sabzi, chicken and losing weight, I was like, this sounds like a deal, man. I can do something like this. I love eating.'

'Wow, she is going to be easy,' I thought to myself. (Easy is my term for sorted people, for those who have already made up their mind to eat right.)

The challenge was Bebo's long working hours and the many on location shoots she needed to do. Unlike what we are led to believe, actors actually lead a very tough, almost middle class life.

'Look I have lot of outdoors now. And I am a vegetarian so my options are limited when I travel, and sometimes I get so hungry, I really don't know what to eat.' She also had long working days, which were also a challenge for changing eating habits.

I assured Bebo that we would plan the diet around her schedule, explained the 4 principles, and worked out a plan for her. Luckily, she was in Mumbai in the first two weeks, so we had the home ground advantage.

'Are you sure I will lose weight on this? This is just so much more than what I eat!'

From eating 2 to 3 times a day, Kareena's diet changed to eating up to 8 times a day. Obviously this included all her favourites: paratha, poha, cheese, paneer, etc. 'I am going to give it my 100%', she assured me.'

'Plan for everything in advance,' I warned. 'Stock up your stores and watch your timing to the T'.

'I will be bang on,' said Bebo. And she was. Totally.

I met her after 2 weeks. 'I am looking like a stick,' she announced. 'I am loving this. I am never hungry. After every 2 hours, I get this feeling that it's time to eat and I eat little and feel very happy and satisfied. So new for me. I am used to not feeling hungry and then dabaoing when I see food. Everybody is telling me how much weight I have lost.'

She had barely lost 2 kilos, but she was totally supportive and appreciative of herself and the efforts that she was putting into eating right and eating on time. This was new to me. I usually have to lecture people on learning to appreciate their bodies. I was used to people losing as much as 30 kilos on the diet, yet remaining unappreciative of themselves and their bodies.

And irrespective of the weight they lost or the sizes they dropped, nobody had ever said to me that they were looking like sticks. Most people pointed out to 'problem areas' when told they were looking leaner.

Bebo was already looking and feeling great. Weight loss is never on my mind, and it was not on her mind either. She has from day 1 focussed on the basics: eat right, eat on time, plan and carry meals so that there is no panic situation, workout 3 days a week.

Her eating habits, meal composition and the size of her meals had changed. Bebo's digestive system was feeling relaxed and happy. Her body, face, skin, hair looked better than ever. When she shot for the song 'Its Rocking' in the film *Kya Love Story Hai*, the media went into a frenzy and called her anorexic. (It's just too tough for most people to believe that correct eating and working out regularly can change and transform bodies.) While the people that she worked with and those who were present on the sets were seeing her eat all the time (in fact, eating the so called 'fattening' foods), she was already getting the reputation of being a 'sing-dana girl' on the sets.

'*Jab We Met* was a landmark because the audiences loved her in the movie and the character she played. Everybody wanted to take the chulbuli train-catching Sikhni from Bhatinda, Geet home. She was dressed mostly in Patiala salwars, long kurtas and longer skirts. But the fact that she was 'covered' on screen didn't deter her from watching her diet. By this time she had adopted the diet and its 4 principles as a way of life. All that changed was her meal options as Geet made her journey from Rajasthan to Punjab to Himachal. She was feeling healthier and nourished from within. And you can see it too: in 'Mauja hi mauja' she looks leaner than in 'Its Rocking'.

The real test came in September 2007 when she

had to shoot in Ladakh for *Tashan*. The original bikini shot was planned in Pangong Tso, a high altitude salt lake. (Second highest in the world. It's on the border of India and China and amongst my favourite places in the world.) I was very excited about the bikini shot, and Bebo was in great shape. However when I met her for planning her Ladakh diet, she was kind of nervous. It was a long schedule in Ladakh and she worried it would affect her diet.

'Will I get any vegetarian food in Ladakh? I hope I don't mess up all my hard work just because I don't get proper food.'

'Don't worry Bebo, Ladakh is predominantly vegetarian because of Buddhism and you will love their food, their pudina and butter chais,' I reassured her. Ladakhi cuisine is amazing, and Leh has some really good eating places—the pizzas especially are to die for.

Kareena's meal 1 would start at 7 am because she would wake up by 6.45 am to report on time for her shoots. She was very happy to know that Ladakh was vegetarian because that increased her meal options. Of course, to be on the safer side she took her soy milk and peanuts with her.

Ladakh tends to be very sunny and windy in the day and extremely cold in the nights. During her shoot she was eating momos and thukpa for lunch, yak and goat cheese as in between meals, etc. basically the yummiest of local produce and cuisines. What makes Kareena what she is, is the fact that once she believes in something she never questions it. She puts her full faith into it and gives it everything she has. So while others speculated how and why was she eating carb rich and therefore 'fattening' momos and thukpas along with the fat rich and therefore 'fattening' cheese, she relished every bite of them. It went with her philosophy of eating 'real' food. Bebo continued to look and get leaner and healthier.

The bikini shot eventually didn't happen in Ladakh; it was shot in Greece instead. Here the vegetarian options were limited. Mostly we had to stick to peas, beans, rice, stuffed tomatoes and capsicum, feta cheese and fruit yogurt (all local produce). Again, Bebo's diet consisted of foods which were considered 'fattening' yet what was reported in the media was an 'orange juice diet'. After the song 'Chaliya Chaliya' and the tastefully shot bikini scene (easily the best till date), her lean look and her outfits made the press speculation around anorexia and orange juice diets even stronger. Though I was interviewed prime time on numerous channels, journalists with unhealthy body compositions (sorry, they really don't take care of themselves) were not ready to accept that she was 'eating'. Everybody felt that only not eating (or at the most having only orange juice) was the way to get as lean as Kareena. (I am using the word lean because she looks healthy and toned, not drained and skinny).

Her body didn't get lean overnight for 'Chaliya chaliya' or the bikini shot. By the time she'd shot for these she had watched her diet for over 6 months. She had been working out for more than 5 years with great consistency. (She never got bored of working out. She tried different exercises, from weight training, to treadmills, to power yoga.) Her body was already intelligent; people who workout regularly have cells that are 'smarter' or more 'intelligent' than people who don't exercise. This means that the cells, enzymes, and hormones when stimulated with the right supply of nutrients (through eating right at the right time) quickly learn to let go of fat stores, improve metabolic rate, and work at increasing lean tissue (stronger bones and denser muscles). A body which has not worked out or has no interest in working out takes a longer time to respond to fat loss, because the cells are not very receptive or smart.

Kareena was exactly of the same body composition, or only marginally different during the shooting of *Tashan*, from her *Jab We Met* days. But the character she played in *Tashan* was way different from Geet. Here she was not bubbly girl-next-door, she had shades of grey. Her styling, clothes, hair, makeup, reflected this. Gone were the long kurtas and Patiala salwars. Enter short skirts, bare midriffs, dark kohl, curly hair and the bikini.

'Oh, she has really lost weight,' the world noticed. 'She is so thin now, size zero.' But she was the exact same size for *Jab We Met*. If there was any difference it was in the clothes, character and the way she was shot.

Her body had changed from 'Yeh Mera Dil' to 'Its Rocking' to 'Mauja hi Mauja' to 'Chaliya Chaliya', and had done so at a slow, steady, consistent pace. Nobody seemed to notice. For them she was 'fat' in 'Yeh Mera Dil' and 'super thin' in 'Chaliya'. Kareena has been accused of not eating, and nothing can be further from the truth. The only reality is: eat right and at the right time, workout at least 3 times a week and your body will change.

Kareena has made eating right fashionable. More and more people are now waking up to the fact that if she has remained lean for more than a year and worked nonstop (she has one of the busiest schedules in the industry) there has to be something more solid and real to her weight loss than the whole orange juice and starvation theory. (Orange juice; nobody can stay on it for more than 3 days, and certainly no one can shoot having had only orange juice. And eating little or nothing in 3 days never leads to a fab body.)

Through the media furore, Bebo didn't give a damn about what the world was saying, whether they called her fat or thin, and followed her heart. She knows looking lean and staying healthy is a lifelong commitment. She has made it. She is the face of my 'Eat local, think global' philosophy.

PS: Recently, when Bebo shot for *Kambakht Ishq* in Venice, she ate pasta, cheese and olives, again considered 'fattening'. Her stylist and the writer of her movie went on the diet after they saw her eating 'everything' in Venice. According to me, dieting is fun. Eating is comforting, we really don't need to let go of it to get lean. Today, for all the girls on the sets of *Kambakht Ishq* it's fun time. They all take their 2 hour break and eat what they are supposed to; peanuts, sprouts, dal khichdi, etc according to their individual plans. They are enjoying being on the diet. So can you.

Size zero

Breaking news: Bebo bani size zero! Kaise kar dikhaya Kareena ne yeh Karishma?

Heard of vanity sizing? It's the practice of labelling your clothes smaller than the actual size so that you feel good about fitting into 'oh smaller than I thought' size. (Don't we all love to fit in a dress smaller than our size?) It's a kickass marketing strategy to get women to buy more (basically encourage them to SPEND more).

Size zero gained prominence in the media after the famous 'size zero ban' at the Madrid Fashion Week. (This, interestingly, had to do with BMI of models and not with the clothing size they wore at the fashion week. Once again focussed only on weight and height and nothing to do with fitness or body composition.)

As for me, I quickly googled size zero when I saw the above mentioned breaking news. I am a ghat, so have very little to do with style, clothes, fashion, etc. But now I am a walking encyclopedia on size zero. This is what it is: size zero is a US clothing size, equivalent of a UK 4 or Europe 30. This clothing size was not invented to fit a new emerging class of super slim celebrities or models, just plain vanity sizing.

Now size zero between me and Bebo is a joke: she sucks her cheeks in, pouts and says, 'Ruj, I want to be size zero!'

2   It's non-negotiable: exercise as a part of your life

Is exercising a must? Yes, it's a must. Our body, this wonderful creation of God, was designed for activity. Walking, running, twisting, jumping, etc. Just like the way man created this wonderful machine called the car. Cars were designed for driving.

Here's a story for you. Once upon a time there were 2 cars parked next to each other: a Maruti 800 and a Mercedes Benz. The Maruti would go for drives almost every day at least for 30 minutes. The Benz preferred to stay parked. Of course, she would get regular waxing, cleaning, etc and looked fab from outside. Passers by would stop and give her a second look. Then, after 3 years, terror struck on the coast of Mumbai, and both cars had to move to a safe place. The Maruti could quickly start and get to a safer place. The Benz, on the other hand, had a tough time just getting started; she looked great from the outside but inside she was rusting from lack of activity. Thanks to the spirit of Mumbai, some passers by pushed it so that she could start herself and she only barely managed to get to a safe place.

I don't have anything for Maruti or anything against Merc. I am just saying that irrespective of the make, the cost, the status or the reputation, driving is the car's primary function or nityam dharma. A car which is driven with love and care, looks great not just from the outside but feels great from the inside too. The driver (in-dweller) of the car can stay in touch with the car's feelings, problems, etc only if its driven regularly. As the car gets driven regularly, it finds the space to communicate openly with the in-dweller or driver: 'Hey, I am running out of petrol'; 'I think my brake oil is low'; 'Hmm, I love this road'; 'Ouch, don't overtake like that, please' etc. Without the act of driving, there is no space or scope for communication.

Similarly, our body, irrespective of the genetics (car make) that it is born with (naturally thin/will get fat at a later age/still look good at 50, etc) and income level it enjoys (some of us stay in match boxes, others in bungalows, etc), needs exercise and activity. When you exercise, the body gets the chance to communicate with the in-dweller. ('I think I should finish eating by 8 pm'; 'Ouch, my knee hurts in this position'; 'Wow, I love running'; 'Am I looking bloated', etc). This communication gives us a chance to tread the path of health, correct our mistakes; reaffirms our belief in eating correctly and at the right time. Without this communication there is not much happiness and much less peace.

So exercising, whatever your age, status, body weight, salary, gender, etc is a must. The physical body or the 'ananmaya kosha' needs to workout. It's pretty simple: if you are breathing, you need to exercise. Research is increasingly pointing out that even those amongst us who have different abilities need a workout. (The gyms that I run in 2 colleges in Mumbai, Ruia & SIES, have some members who have overcome serious challenges of sight, hearing, mobility, etc to keep fit. My trainers love training them because they are among the most sincere and dedicated members we have.) So if you are 'normal', hello! Wake up and exercise. Hospitals and doctors are increasingly using physiotherapy as one of the major post operative procedures. It simply means activity. (Why doctors might not believe in activity or exercise as a means of staying healthy or injury prevention, pre-surgery is a mystery).

Which exercise you choose as means to keeping fit is a completely personal choice. A lot of what you prefer doing: yoga, weight training, running, swimming, etc has to do with your temperament, what you discovered first or what your friends and family believe in or recommend. All forms of exercise lead you to the same path, that of health, vitality and peace. The benefits of exercise go way beyond losing weight or losing inches. It will improve muscle and bone density, heart and lung function, lower blood pressure, stabilise blood sugar and make you agile, faster and stronger.

But this happens only if you eat right and keep the right attitude towards life and exercise itself. Adopting exercise just as a means to losing weight can be detrimental to health, because you will risk doing too much in too little time. Once you commit yourself to regular workouts, weight loss will just happen, with the right diet. Putting time constraints on results often takes the fun and joy out of exercise.

Before embarking on a fitness programme make sure that you go through a preliminary fitness test. This is a non-invasive test which measures your body composition, flexibility, strength and endurance. A basic knowledge of these parameters is important before starting on a fitness plan.

Like MSD once said in an interview, 'The most important part of fitness is REST'. Workouts, whether you run, weight train, do aerobics, spin or swim, are catabolic in their very nature. Which means that every time you exercise there is microscopic wear and tear to your muscle. Exercise actually breaks your body down. Just like driving will cause wear and tear of the car, but keeping it parked all the time will destroy it. However, the difference is that the human body is blessed with a process called adaptation: when exercise provides the right stimuli (wear and tear) the body's ability to adapt kicks in. So with the help of right nutrients (that come through food), water and rest, the body rebuilds what has gotten broken down during exercise. That way when you do the same workout the next time, it causes less or no damage.

Then, for your body to keep learning, you have to increase the stimuli. So from running 2 kilometres you run 3 kilometres, from 2 rounds of surya namaskar you go to 3, or from 2 pounds on the dumbbell curl you go to 3. You increase the stimuli, create new wear and tear in the body, and then use all the nutrients in your body and adequate rest to learn or adapt from that stimuli, so you keep growing, getting stronger, fitter, leaner with each passing day.

Of course, when you commit to exercise you must ensure that you seek the advice of the right professional. When you meet a trainer, ask her about her qualifications, experience, etc. Discuss your problems with her, gauge whether she understands you correctly, puts your concerns to rest and suggests a good programme. Make sure the programme is personalised to your needs, fitness levels (or lack of them), timings and goals. Most importantly, it must provide for adequate recovery time. Just like you should not trust a nutritionist who doesn't believe in exercise, you should not trust a trainer who doesn't believe in eating right. Your trainer (whether or not she can speak in English) should have sound knowledge on exercise physiology, kinesiology, biomechanics, injury prevention and should look in good shape. A trainer should be able to teach you the correct form or technique of exercise and should help you have a realistic view in terms of how soon you can see 'results'. But trust me, 'results' start happening from minute 1 of exercise, whether you see them or not. So please don't grudge your body for taking time, instead encourage it to take all the time in the world.

Go ahead and choose the exercise you want to commit yourself to it. A lot of people I meet are scared to exercise because they feel they will lose all the benefits of exercise when they stop exercising.

Of course **fitness is a perishable entity, it's not something that can be stored forever.** But then why should you ever stop exercising? Exercising is crucial to the body, just like driving is to the car. So go ahead and workout. Your body will be able to maintain fitness levels for up to 3 weeks without stimuli, after which it will start letting go of its fitness levels. Our body works by one principle, remember: 'Use it or lose it'.

About 5 years ago, each one of us had at least 10 phone numbers by heart. Enter mobile phones and we don't remember our partner's number, or work or home numbers. The brain has lost its power to recollect because we are just not using it for this anymore. So if there is no reason to use fitness then you might as well lose it; or at least that's what our body believes. The good news here is that just like the brain, muscle has memory too. So if you take to exercise even after a long, long gap, your muscles will return to the fitness levels you stopped at because it will remember them. Just like a poem you knew in school; if you hear somebody recite the first 4 lines, your memory will be refreshed and you can join in from the 5th or 6th line.

And if you are tired of weight training, take to cycling. Bored of that? Take to running. But remember that exercise is a lifelong commitment. So you will need to keep at it, in one way or another.

'Will exercise cause injuries?' is like asking, 'Will driving cause accidents?' Well, not if you are not drinking and driving, not driving when you are tired and sleepy, following all the traffic rules, not driving in a fit of rage and taking care of the body parts of your car; enough petrol, brake oil, coolant, etc. So if you follow all the rules, you can have a safe drive and enjoy your car. Similarly, working out when not sick, tired or sleepy, eating right before and after exercise, drinking enough water, warming up, cooling down, stretching, using the right techniques, etc will not injure your body. But when you overdo exercise and don't eat or rest enough, it's like an accident. You can see the damage but you can't make out what caused it; too much exercise, too little food, lack of sleep, or something else?

On the other hand, doing too little exercise is a pure waste of time and energy. Every time you exercise, it should challenge the body's current fitness levels. This is called 'the progressive over load' principle. Which means every day you teach your body a little bit, so that it continues to learn and remain interested in exercise. Just like after you learn the alphabet you progress to words and then to sentences. If you are taught alphabets every single day, you will lose interest in them. And if you are taught sentences on day 1, you will decide that they are just not right for you. So an exercise should follow a proper step up plan and never under work you or overdo.

Is one form of exercise better than another? No. Do what you enjoy doing. Not because some celebrity endorses it, or because it's a great calorie burner, or anything else as slight. Workouts are after all a way of overcoming our body's limitations. Just make sure that your trainer understands your strengths and limitations, and the strengths and limitations of the form of exercise that he or she preaches and practices. The essence of all forms of exercise is one, the differences are only superficial. All forms of exercise should help you get closer to yourself, allow your body to communicate with you, and help you overcome the limitations of your body. A good religious or spiritual leader helps you understand your religion better, shows you how to adapt the principles of the religion to your daily living depending on your surroundings, and knows that all religions lead to the same goal. A fundamentalist leader, though, has poor knowledge about his own religion and is therefore incapable of guiding you onto the right path. Similarly, a trainer who looks down on other forms of exercise other than those she preaches has limited understanding of her own form of exercise. All exercises lead to the same goal: that of health, fitness and peace.

Exercise myths

Weight training

Myth: the biggest myth about weight training is that you will develop muscles or become a body builder if you start. Have you ever picked up a cricket bat and played on a Sunday and feared that if you continue playing you may turn into Sachin

Tendulkar? Sounds stupid? So does this.

Reality: training in the gym will only make your bones denser, joints, tendons and ligaments stronger, and muscles bigger (men) or toned (women). As your body develops stronger bones and muscles, it learns to become an effective fat burning machine. Muscle and bone are active tissues, so they burn more fat for you.

Recommendation: train at least twice a week for not more than 60 minutes. If you are suffering from joint pains or have arthritis or osteoporosis in the family, you should definitely invest time and money in a good trainer and gym. Always have your post workout meal of high GI and protein within 20 minutes.

Yoga

Myth: you have to give up on sex if you start yoga. This is one of the most popular myths fitness professionals have to hear. My God! Nothing could be further away from the truth. Lord Shiva, the first guru of yoga was a complete family man; 'Hum do hamare do.'

Reality: yoga is about being in control of your body, mind and senses. It encourages having a balanced and disciplined approach towards life. Bramhacharya is not abstinence from sex but conduct (including sexual conduct) which will bring you closer to reality or your true self. So go ahead and do your suryanamaskars and asanas. If it does affect your sex life, trust me it's only going to be only for the better.

Recommendation: yoga is a restorative form of physical exercise which also works at calming your nerves and senses. You can do yoga daily. Keep your stomach relatively empty before you start with the postures and eat a healthy meal post your yoga class.

Walking

Myth: walking is much safer than running. I think walking is the most overrated exercise. In India it is as much of a phenomenon as the big fat Indian wedding. Just like at the wedding, everybody who walks is fat, hairy, gaudy and loud. Men in large groups wearing shorts and protruding bellies, women mostly in pairs (they're mostly with another woman) in salwars and shoes; lastly, a Maruti van outside the park selling juices in all colours and if you are a regular some complimentary moong shots.

Reality: walking in the same park, doing the same rounds, with the same people, conversing about the same topics—share bazaar, the economy, recipes, daughters-in-law, state of the city—will not improve anybody's fitness levels (and that's why it is a dangerous waste of time and energy). Some people walk for years together and see no benefit at all. These obsessive walkers may occasionally use the gyms where they walk some more on the treadmill and instead of chatting with friends, change channels on the TV screen. Others indulge in some perverted forms of breathing and call it prananayam. Walking is great but only if it provides a challenge to your body. Try the talk test. If you can't talk at all, you're walking or running too fast. If you can sing, then you're too slow. If you are walking properly, you'll only be able to talk with difficulty and most certainly won't be able to gossip.

Recommendation: Try running for 30 minutes at a stretch. If you can't, try running a couple of rounds instead of just walking. You can start with as little as a 30 second run and build up slowly to 3 to 13 minutes over few months. Try interval training; run for a while, then walk, and keep repeating this cycle. Always invest in good shoes, and stretch before and after the run.

3   DIY diet recall

Day 1			
Time	**Food/drink with quantity**	**Activity recall**	**Workout**

Day 2			
Time	Food/drink with quantity	Activity recall	Workout

Day 3			
Time	Food/drink with quantity	Activity recall	Workout

Acknowledgements

This book would not have been possible without the help, support, inspiration and sacrifice of many people around me. And at the cost of making it sound like a film award acceptance speech I would like to thank:

- All my 'diet clients' who supported me wholeheartedly during my marathon book writing and for putting up with my switched off cell phone/no appointments for 2 months/ sms and email replies after 2 days. And also for reassuring me with 'Don't know about others but I will definitely buy your book.'
- My entire team at Ruia and SIES college gyms for actually working better when the boss was not around. And for making excuses about my absence with the gym members.
- My marathon runners for being patient and 'totally ok' about me not putting up the Sunday long run analysis as late as Monday evenings.
- My trainer friends and yoga teachers for sharing some really interesting diet stories and myths with me.
- The entire staff of Costa Coffee, Oshiwara, where I wrote most of the book.

- My parents and my sister, Ankita, for always being there for me.
- My workaholic editor Chiki, for her encouragement and retaining what I thought is essential for my book even when she thought otherwise.

And a very special thanks to my partner, GP, without whom this book would 'not quite be there'.

A note on the author

Rujuta Diwekar works out of Mumbai, practises yoga in Rishikesh, ideates in Uttarkashi and treks in rest of the Indian Himalaya. For over a decade she has worked with people from all walks of life on fitness and diet related issues. Her celebrity clients include Kareena Kapoor, Anil Ambani, Saif Ali Khan, Konkona Sen and Preity Zinta. Amongst the few qualified sports science and nutrition experts in the country today, she has redefined dieting with her holistic approach towards a healthy lifestyle.

www.rujutadiwekar.com